MW00343290

Natural Garden Style

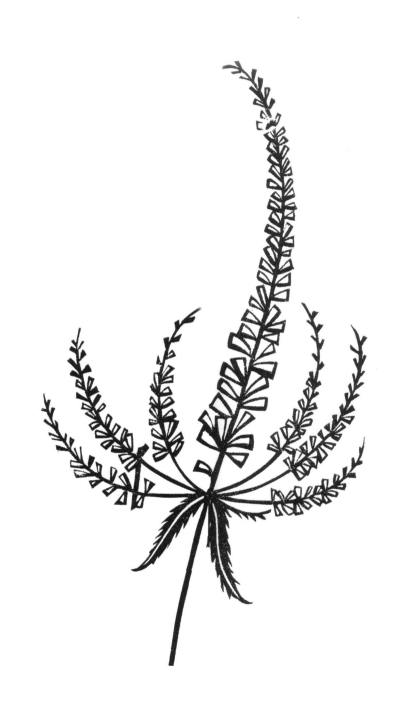

Noël Kingsbury

Photography by
Nicola Browne

Natural Garden Style

Gardening Inspired by Nature

MERRELL
LONDON · NEW YORK

Contents

Introduction

PEOPLE APPRECIATE AND USE THEIR GARDENS for many reasons. A garden might be a place in which to relax or entertain, or somewhere to grow fruit and vegetables or cut flowers for the house. For many it is a safe playground for children. Those with a love of plants can make their gardens into botanical treasure troves. Increasingly, though, the garden is becoming a place in which to appreciate and celebrate nature.

Urban gardeners, particularly, may seek to welcome nature into their gardens, but perhaps do not realize just how successful that can be. One of the aims of this book is to show how it is possible. In country areas, too, the increasingly industrial scale of agriculture is making the garden a valued home for nature, while gardeners in comparatively unspoiled rural areas, where nature has plenty of room of its own, often want a garden to have a sense of belonging to its local environment.

A feeling that we are out of touch with nature is widespread. At the beginning of the twenty-first century we have begun to realize just how much damage the human race has done to the natural world, at the same time recognizing that we possess the resources and understanding to do something about it. At the private and individual level one thing we can do is to welcome nature back into our gardens. The widespread and very popular desire to be 'natural' in the garden is part and parcel of a much greater sense of unease about the way the human race has been managing (or mismanaging) the world; it is also about optimism and hope: that as private individuals we can do something in our own personal spaces to create a more harmonious relationship with the natural world.

This book is about making natural-style gardens. Central to such gardens are plants, preferably those that have some hint of the wild about them. I propose to discuss plants in the context of their natural habitats,

as we are used to thinking about garden plants on their own, or as design elements to be combined according to aesthetic judgements. In nature, different plant species combine to form recognizable and relatively predictable communities. Bringing nature into the garden must involve learning about these plant communities and about the particular combinations of light, moisture and fertility that favour some but not others. Developing a feeling for the link between environment and plant is an important part of creating a garden that minimizes not only maintenance but also irrigation, inputs of fertilizer or indeed fuel for the lawnmower. A natural-style garden, in other words, is a more sustainable garden.

Natural-style gardening is also about celebrating natural materials. There is a big divide in the garden-design world between those who see design as basically about construction and 'hard' materials, and those who focus on plants. Here I take the line that, although plants may come first, there is always a need for hard materials – for paths, benches, retaining walls, fences – and that natural ones will be not only more consistent with the ethos and the look of the garden but also more sustainable.

ROMANCE AND REALISM

No garden is ever really 'natural'. Leave a garden to the forces of nature and the result will nearly always be a tangled mess of vegetation that will give little joy to anyone other than a dedicated naturalist (and preferably one interested in weed floras). We have to be honest. What we want from a patch of land and what nature would do with it, given half a chance, are very different. The nature we want in our gardens is a refined and tidied-up version, preferably one that is pretty and keeps us interested for as much of the year as possible. It will inevitably be a compromise, which is not a bad thing for nature either. Gardens can often be very good places for biodiversity; those who have surveyed garden insects,

Previous page Green roofs are a new technology aimed at minimizing a range of human impacts on the environment. They also help to insulate buildings, particularly from excessive summer heat. In this one by Jean Kling, several species of sedum are used, along with chives (*Allium schoenoprasum*). The substrate (artificial soil substitute) here is approximately 5 cm (2 in) deep. Deeper substrates can support richer floras; for example, a 10–12-cm (4–5-in) layer is enough for a wild-flower-rich dry-meadow flora.

Opposite The seed heads of *Echinacea purpurea* stand out against paler grasses in the Lurie Garden by Piet Oudolf in Chicago's Millennium Park, bringing interest to a time of year when there are relatively few flowers. Nature in the city brings an emotional respite to humans, but vital habitats and resources for birds and other wildlife.

for example, spending hours on hands and knees capturing and counting the flies, bugs and weevils that the rest of us disregard, report that the average suburban garden is astonishingly biodiverse – more so, indeed, than heavily managed farmland. Very often, when unmanaged nature takes over from humanity on abandoned land the vegetation is dominated by a limited number of very aggressive species (often not even regional natives). It may seem an irony, but nature managed can support more species than nature unmanaged. It is very important to remember this when we consider how we manage our natural-style gardens.

Looking beyond the garden, and indeed well beyond the city boundary, much of what we call 'nature' is not natural either, but the result of centuries or millennia of human intervention. Meadows, full of wild flowers in early summer, are a product of annual mowing and occasional grazing by sheep, cattle or other livestock. Leave a meadow uncut for ten years and the first tree seedlings will appear; leave it for fifty years and the original wild-flower flora will all but vanish. Even much of the once vast prairie of the American Midwest is now known to be 'unnatural': the result of Native Americans burning the grass to promote good grazing for buffalo.

If much natural landscape is not at all natural, but the result of many years' stewardship, of partnership between humanity and nature, then 'cultured landscape' is a more accurate term. It is important to recognize this as we approach the task of making our gardens seem more natural places. The 'natural garden' has been the target of much romantic writing and misconception. Myths have grown up, the seeds of misunderstandings and misconceptions very often sown by those whose understanding of nature is a romantic one, untempered by the realism of the science of the natural world. It is perhaps best to examine some of these myths before going any further.

Curves and straight lines

Straight lines in nature are rare, and it is a commonplace that a natural garden should eschew them as much as possible, favouring instead curves and bends, with one habitat or planting changing subtly and gradually into another. But is a bird seeking a nesting site going to worry about whether the shrubs in your garden are in straight lines? Of course not.

It is partly, but not entirely, true that an absence of straight lines and geometry will make a garden look more informal and relaxed, and therefore natural. Sometimes a straight line or a neatly clipped hedge can create a spark, emphasizing the 'naturalness' of the rest of the garden – a 'creative tension', in other words. Sometimes order is necessary to illustrate intention: neatly mown paths through long grass point out to onlookers that the length of the grass is intended and not the result of laziness or a broken-down mower. Indeed, one of the most potent examples of creative tension in the garden is the juxtaposition of neatly clipped topiary with long meadow grass.

A more pertinent problem than curvy lines and shapes is that of gradation. Humanity tends to favour clear contrasts and divisions between features of the environment. As an example, think of the clear boundary between a conventional flower border and a mown lawn, or the trees rising out of mown grass in many public parks. Such clear and sudden boundaries are profoundly unnatural, and do biodiversity no favours. Consider how a small animal is going to get from the ground into a tree without being seen by a possible predator; it is very difficult if there is no intermediary layer of sheltering vegetation. I look at this subject in more detail later (see page 20).

Native and non-native plants

Much good has come of movements in many parts of the world to encourage the growing of locally native plants, in particular through their championing of plants that have been otherwise disregarded. In some cases these species can play an important part in supporting biodiversity, for example by being food sources for specialist insect species. In northern Europe, the common English oak (Quercus robur) can feed more than 200 insect species, but American species of oak support only a handful; the converse is also true, and Q. robur supports little in America, while native species feed abundant wildlife. But this is not to say that only natives support wildlife. Many non-native species are exceptionally good for fauna: Buddleja davidii, for example, is the most wonderful source of nectar for butterflies in North American and European gardens, yet is a native of China. As a general rule, the more diverse the flora in your garden, the more it will benefit wildlife.

Organic gardening methods

The 'organic' philosophy evolved in the early twentieth century from mysticism rather than science. It seeks to avoid the use of all 'artificial' chemicals in the garden, but shows little consistency in defining what 'artificial' is. In fact, as I hope to show in this book, chemical remedies for garden problems are generally unnecessary. In seeking to garden in tune with nature, we aim to avoid feeding the soil – there are plenty of beautiful plant species that will flourish on poor soil – so no need for fertilizers. Rich, diverse and slightly wild-looking plantings have so much visual interest that the odd plant with mildew or holes in its leaves from caterpillars is rarely a problem – so no need for pesticides.

Weeds, however, especially if they are aggressive and invasive non-native aliens, are a problem in more and more regions of the globe. An important lesson of plant ecological science is that high-resource environments (with plentiful fertility and moisture) tend to be dominated by very few species, usually strongly spreading

Wild gardening does not have to exclude geometry. These trees in a Warwickshire garden by Dan Pearson are planted on a grid, and their underplanting of a sedge, Carex pendula, is arranged in squares. Regular mowing of the grass paths ensures that the sedge (a strongly spreading species) does not stray. Herbaceous planting does compete with the roots of young trees, so it is very important that the trees are not underplanted until well established.

ones. Weed growth, particularly on fertile soils, is the greatest impediment to natural-style gardening; there are many species that, given the proverbial inch, will take a mile. Careful and targeted use of weedkillers makes all the difference in the early stages of garden-making, but the need for their use tails off rapidly as gardens mature. There are some weedkillers that are very safe and biodegrade rapidly, so do not be afraid to use them. The irony is that good use of chemical herbicides can be very effective in promoting the diverse, species-rich gardens so beneficial for biodiversity.

What is natural is good and safe

This is what you are meant to think when your eye lights on the innumerable products in the supermarket or garden centre adorned with the word 'natural'. The wholesale takeover of the word by both the corporate sector and the New Age movement has meant that it has become one of the most abused words in the English language. That 'natural' is not necessarily safe is powerfully illustrated by the bewildering range of toxins found in poisonous berries and plants.

So much of what we do in our everyday lives is deeply unnatural, and that is what makes us human. Reading this book is an unnatural activity, as is driving or cycling to the bookshop to buy it. I have consequently used the word 'natural' as little as possible in this book. Far more useful is to think about sustainability in practice, and natural style in design. To talk of natural-style gardens implies that we are the designers but we take nature for our muse – we are not trying to copy it.

SUSTAINABILITY

Key to natural-style gardening is the subject of sustainability. This touches on what has become a distinctive feature of the modern garden world: a concern with what are, at heart, ethical issues.

Sustainability is essentially about minimizing the input needed to create and maintain a garden: stone and cement for paths, fertilizer and composts for soil improvement, plastic for pond lining, and so on; and about minimizing harmful output: toxic chemical residues, pollution from petrol-driven engines, and the energy involved in producing and transporting everything from plants to labels. Sustainability is primarily about making technical decisions informed by ethical goals. Such decisions must be based on objective facts, not ideological, political or romantic notions of what 'feels right'.

Anyone interested in natural-style gardening will almost certainly be deeply concerned with sustainability. The desire to nurture nature in the garden or evoke natural environments nearly always goes hand-in-hand with a desire to conserve natural habitats elsewhere in the world and to minimize damage to the planet as a whole. Deciding what really is sustainable, however, can be difficult – there is often no clear black-and-white, right-or-wrong way. Ambiguities and compromises have to be accepted, and trade-offs where no course of action is truly sustainable have to be recognized.

It is useful to consider a few examples. One is transport miles. This is a measure of how much energy has been used to move a product from its place of origin to its final place of use or installation. Stone shipped from India or China would surely appear to involve far more transport miles, for example, than a product sourced locally. This applies to plants, too. A relatively

A stylized version of naturalistic planting, where variation has been decreased and single-variety blocks used to reduce maintenance. The use of grasses, however, evokes wild landscapes. This is Dan Pearson's garden at Broughton Hall in Yorkshire.

recent development is the shipping of plants over vast distances. If the plants are small and light, such as the cuttings produced in Kenya and flown out for growing on in Holland, then that is of little account, but the recent fashion for garden centres and nurseries to sell extra-large trees and shrubs, often involving transport over long distances, is certainly a contributor to congestion on roads and the consumption of fossil fuels. In fact, mature and semi-mature trees and shrubs do not necessarily adapt well to their new homes, or establish very slowly, so the whole exercise is often a waste of money. The long-distance shipping of products that are then marketed as 'eco-friendly' is a particular absurdity – coir, which is derived from coconut bark and used for making compost, is a good example.

Another instance of the difficulty of making clear-cut decisions about sustainability concerns weed clearance. It is fundamentally important to eliminate aggressive, unwanted species from land before making a garden. In most cases these weeds have established their position of dominance through human activity, so their removal in order to create a naturalistic garden is not such an anomaly. The conventional technique of removing them with chemical herbicides is opposed by

Right At Broughton Hall, Dan Pearson's natural-style gardening aims at subtle planting effects, relying on foliage colour and texture and a scattering of flowers rather more than bold masses of bright colour. But as with any garden, long-flowering plants are much appreciated. Here are two of the best: *Verbena bonariensis* (top, foreground) and *Erysimum* 'Bowles's Mauve' (both images, centre). Both flourish on infertile soils.

Opposite One way to make the garden as near to a natural space as possible is to fill every gap with plants. Remember that nature abhors a vacuum! Ground-cover plants are particularly useful for this purpose, and provide vital low-level invertebrate habitat, contributing to the numbers of larger and more attractive wildlife, such as birds. Combining several different species will create an effect that is more interesting visually and, in general, more biodiverse, too. This is Tom Vanderpoel's garden in Illinois.

many, despite an excellent safety record for many such products and an absence of evidence of environmental damage for many of the chemicals concerned. The alternative is to use black plastic sheeting or old carpet to smother weeds over the course of a growing season: a very effective method, but one that leaves behind a pile of unusable plastic or carpet. What seems at first to be an admirably 'chemical-free' solution can, in practice, involve an even greater consumption of energy and resources, and also present disposal problems.

WILD PLANTS AND GARDEN PLANTS

The plants grown in gardens fall into two categories: species that are more or less identical to their wild ancestors; and cultivated varieties, which are to some extent 'man-made'. The latter type covers a wide range. It includes simple selections of plants made from the wild and propagated to maintain particular desired characteristics – *Euphorbia dulcis* 'Chameleon', for example, is a dark form of a common wild plant, found by chance in a ditch in France – as well as plants that have been in cultivation for centuries and undergone a huge number of genetic changes (hybrid roses – desirable to the human eye and good for the nursery business but very unnatural-looking – are a good example).

Highly bred plants are often very different from naturally occurring wild species. They usually have larger flowers, or at least a higher proportion of flower to leaf, with the result that, compared with their wild ancestors, they lack a natural grace and poise. Double flowers are common among garden plants, but rare among wild plants; often they are sterile, or do not contain nectar, in which case they will not attract or feed bees or other insects. It is not just flowers that have attracted the attention of breeders down the centuries. Variegated or coloured foliage has always been popular, and is now perhaps more than ever. Such coloured leaves are

inherently physiologically inefficient, and would probably lead to the plant dying out in the wild.

Whether or not such hybrid plants are desirable is, of course, a personal and subjective decision. But many who wish to create a natural-style garden will feel sympathetic to the idea that such 'artificial' plants either do not belong there, or should appear only in designed features close to the house, to emphasize their cultural, as opposed to natural, heritage.

One of the pleasures of the natural-style garden is the opportunity to enjoy plants that maintain the proportion and balance of wild flowers. A garden dominated by wild or naturally proportioned plants will have a different look from a more traditional one, with its bold masses of bright colours. The natural-style garden will contain a much higher proportion of leaf and stem to flower, and of green to other colours. It will inevitably be more subtle.

Conventional gardens have tended to rely heavily on colour. Many groups of plants include varieties that offer colour variations from the wild plant, but still have the same proportions; but the naturalistic aesthetic also places an emphasis on foliage, plant shape and the look of the plant at those times of year when it would conventionally be regarded as 'off-season'. So, if you wish to make a natural-style garden you will need to think about much more than flower colour – to look at the whole plant, at the angle and thrust of stems, at the texture, colour and shape of leaves and at the appearance of the plant in all seasons. This attention

Seed heads have a beauty of their own, which is missed entirely if the conventional practice of cutting back dead foliage in the autumn is carried out. This is *Phlomis russeliana*, a plant whose ground-covering leaves (evergreen in mild winter climates) make it supremely useful for low-maintenance plantings; its golden–yellow flowers in early summer are followed by these decorative seed heads, sturdy enough to last all winter.

Left This richly textured collection of shrubs in Bonnington Square, London, illustrates how the dense intermingling of plants, which conventional practice has tended to reject, can be very attractive. The distinctive large foliage is that of *Euphorbia mellifera* (lower right), a somewhat tender species that thrives in warm urban environments.

Below Selecting the right plant for difficult situations is vital for making sustainable gardens. In fact, most perennial and woody ornamental plants are more tolerant than we tend to think. *Echinops ritro* is a perennial of rocky places. It is not long-lived, but like nearly all 'less than perennial' plants, it regenerates easily from seed.

to conventionally little-considered aspects of plants can be enlightening, as new sources of interest and beauty are noticed, and plants once considered dull reveal hidden qualities. One important lesson, perhaps, is this: that naturalistic gardening is about not just gardening but also observing and appreciating.

Learning to look at plants anew reveals much, particularly in the spring and autumn. In the spring, as shrubs and herbaceous plants burst into growth, their young leaves are often differently shaped or coloured from their mature foliage, with effects that may be fleeting, but are entrancing. Herbaceous plants in the spring often have shapes that are interesting

in themselves, particularly since many of them become steadily less orderly as the season progresses: the daggers of emerging iris leaves, the neat hemispheres of hardy geraniums, the deep bronze–red of peony leaves. Many of these effects are all too transient, whereas autumn's display of seed heads and fading foliage is usually much longer-lasting. Seed heads, in particular, have great potential to provide interest until well into the winter.

'RIGHT PLANT, RIGHT PLACE'

Fundamental to the natural-style garden is the idea of choosing plants that naturally grow well in the conditions of climate and soil available to them.

Traditionally, gardeners have tended to make great efforts to change the environment of the garden in order to suit particular plants. Much of this was driven by fruit and vegetable gardening, where, broadly speaking, the more you put in, the more you get out – so great efforts were made to improve fertility. The vast majority of ornamental plants simply do not need the soil 'improvement' and increased fertility that much of the gardening industry has, over the years, tried to tell us is necessary. Simply looking at how and where plants grow in nature should teach us that even places where there is nothing that most gardeners would recognize as 'soil' – rocky mountainsides and sand dunes, for example – can support a rich flora.

Those interested in the natural-style garden need to look for plants that will thrive in the conditions their site presents. Fortunately, this has increasingly become a focus of garden reference books, especially as interest in sustainability has grown. Many of the conditions that have traditionally been regarded as 'difficult' simply require a different approach. However problematic conditions are, nature has a beautiful range of plants that will tolerate them. The only exceptions are the dark and dry shade beneath coniferous trees, and those situations where difficulties are primarily man-made, in particular the compressed soils sometimes caused by construction activities around new houses. In the case of the latter, drainage may be necessary, accompanied by the physical break-up of the top layer of soil and the addition of organic matter.

Cold, exposed, windswept situations on infertile and acidic soils can be home to many dwarf shrubs, such as heathers and blueberry relatives, and tough evergreen grasses and sedges. A badly drained clay soil will support such shrubs as willows, along with a host of lush, moisture-loving perennials. A hot, dry slope is perfect for silver- and grey-leaved shrubs, such as cistus and lavender.

Realizing that making a successful and beautiful garden does not involve having to buy and apply fertilizers, composts and soil-improvement products is an important step in learning to create a garden that is not only in balance with its environment but also sustainable. Accepting what the local environment offers means not just saving money but also reducing the use of resources.

LEARNING FROM NATURE

There are big differences between wild plant communities and the way plants are grown in most gardens. Since the former are clearly natural in some way, and the latter not, it makes sense to look at what these differences are, and to consider what they mean for garden design and management. First, it is necessary to distinguish between a genuinely natural environment and an unnatural environment that functions naturally.

Most of the supposedly 'natural' environments with which we are familiar are in no way natural. Anything farmed, such as pastureland, is clearly not. Many apparently unmanaged environments are in fact the result of either management in the past or some kind of human intervention. Many of Britain's heather-covered uplands were covered in forest as recently as a thousand years ago (which is not very long in the lifespan of ecosystems). Much of the thick forest of eastern North America was farmland a century or two ago and, before that, had been partially cleared by Native Americans. The irony is that some of the most biodiverse 'natural' habitats are semi-natural: the (formerly sheep-grazed) grasslands of central and northern Europe for one, the patchwork of prairie–savannah in parts of the North American Midwest for another.

Ecological processes

In a garden, plants are conventionally put into selected positions and expected to stay there. There are usually

gaps between plants so they do not interact. In the wild, plants grow cheek by jowl at a far higher density. A wild-flower meadow or wild prairie is a particularly good place to appreciate the dramatic difference between the garden border and species-rich natural habitat. Get down on your hands and knees and look – there is very little space between the individual plants; indeed, it is all but impossible to tell where one ends and another begins, and trying to see bare earth will almost certainly involve tearing apart a tough-sinewed thatch of leaves, stems and dead growth with your fingertips. Actually finding out how many individual plants there are would take much time and expertise. Easier, but still demanding, is counting species: a British wild-flower meadow can have up to forty-five species per square metre or yard, while steppe (dry grassland) in the Ukraine can contain eighty.

Wild plant communities are always in a state of flux, a constant cycle of plants (and species) spreading, seeding, moving and dying. The population and species mix will change from one year to the next. If a garden border is just minimally managed to control the growth of aggressive weeds or particularly vigorous species, then it too will eventually become denser and more complex, as its components spread and seed. The result may have certain advantages over the conventional border – the dense canopy of vegetation will cover the ground and greatly limit weed infiltration – but it will also have

A clearing in the forest has been planted with a prairie flora. Most of us want our houses to be in the light, and prefer to look at the forest from a distance, rather than being hemmed in by trees. By using native prairie plants in such a situation at his house in Wisconsin, Neil Diboll has imitated the biodiverse and visually rich savannah landscape that once covered much of the American Midwest.

disadvantages: it may look more untidy than many gardeners would want, and certain species are almost certain to take over at the expense of others. But by reducing maintenance to a minimum, the gardener has handed over a large element of the management to natural, ecological processes. The result of doing so with most border combinations would probably result in a mess, but doing some research and planting an ecologically balanced mix of plants should result in a richer and more visually interesting, self-sustaining planting. The lesson for the domestic gardener is that borders of perennials can be managed much more lightly, that plants can be allowed to spread, and that dense plant mixtures may be lower maintenance than more conventionally sparse ones.

Gradations

Take a walk in the woods. Observe. Look at wild plants and how they grow. They grow not only at a far greater density than cultivated plants, but also with a greater level of complexity than can be seen in the garden. Much garden design relies on separating plants and developing strong contrasts (see page 10) and clear boundaries. In nature clear boundaries are rare, and blurring and intermingling are more common. A good way to understand such apparent lack of clarity is to think in terms of *gradations*, whereby one community of plants changes gradually into another. A good example is the gradation from woodland to open conditions in full sun, a progression that can be easily observed along rural paths. Under the trees there is total shade, with a relatively sparse low-level flora of shade-tolerant wild flowers. Towards the edge there is more light, and the flora becomes denser and more varied. The very edge of the wood is often a tangle, as shrubs form a thicket of growth, part of the wood but at the same time benefiting from the bright light. Climbing

plants – rooted in the shade, but clambering up to reach the light – are often a major feature of this area. Around the shrubs is a variety of herbaceous plants, some species typical of shade, others of sun; there are usually grasses, but there is often not enough light for them to dominate as they would in full sun. Beyond is a zone where there is enough light for grasses to take over, and only a limited number of perennials survive. The woodland edge is a transition zone, and like all natural borderlands it is particularly diverse.

One way to think of a garden border is as one of these transition habitats. Potentially it offers a variety of different conditions. Making the most of the range of possibilities and developing its visual potential requires the gardener to consider how plants naturally grow in layers.

Planting in layers

The woodland edge described above provides an example of how plants in nature organize themselves into layers. The ground level is often occupied by low-level creeping species, at least where shade restricts grass growth. Above this are taller herbaceous plants, with some ferns and grasses. Then come herbaceous climbers scrambling to 2–3 m (6–10 ft), although the number of species varies enormously between geographic regions. Shrubs of various sizes occupy the next layer, followed by the tree canopy. Large, woody climbers, such as species of clematis or vine, may clamber to the top of all but the tallest trees.

Gardeners tend to make little use of these vegetation layers. Yet they are a good model both for maximizing interest in small spaces – especially urban gardens, where there are often large expanses of wall – and for providing wildlife habitat. In nature, the multiple layers of vegetation can appear confusing and incoherent; we can find them difficult to 'read'. In the garden, however, this should be less of a problem, since the plants that have been made available by the nursery industry have

Three layers of vegetation are visible in this garden by Jinny Blom: herbaceous perennial, shrub and climber. Notice how the climber acts as a connection between the perennial and shrub layers – a wildlife corridor. The rose is 'Albéric Barbier'.

been chosen for their strong visual impact. In particular, selecting species with good foliage helps to improve coherence and 'readability'.

GARDENING FOR WILDLIFE

One of the greatest changes in attitudes to gardening since the 1990s has been the idea of the garden as wildlife habitat. While many gardeners and their families have always appreciated the presence of birds and butterflies, it is only recently that a strong moral case for encouraging such creatures has been argued. Given how much of the world's space has been concreted over or covered in neat rows of intensively managed crops, many now feel that we have an obligation to maximize the provision of habitat for the species with which we share the earth. Research by biologists has shown that gardens are very good for wildlife, even gardens that are not particularly managed with wildlife in mind. Given how much space private gardens occupy in some urban and all suburban areas, the potential for wildlife is enormous, especially if more gardeners make the effort to think through the design, planting and management of their gardens.

Wildlife, whether feathered, furry or carapaced, requires a number of things: a supply of food and places to feed, shelter and reproduce. A food supply means a food chain; in particular, it means recognizing that the forms of wildlife we value in the garden – primarily birds – are largely dependent on a whole host of wildlife we do not necessarily value, or even like very much: insects and other invertebrates. If we want birds in the garden, then we must have bugs, and lots of them. This does not mean a garden full of troublesome mosquitoes and midges, however; indeed, the presence of a good population of insect-eating birds (and bats) is one of the best ways of keeping noisome insects down.

A complex food chain is the result of a diverse and varied habitat. The more species of plants in a garden, the

greater the resulting biodiversity. Gardeners who like to grow lots of different plants and are good at recognizing opportunities for shoe-horning plants in to form multiple layers of vegetation will have gardens that provide good habitats. Examples of wildlife-friendly multiple layering include ground-cover plants (to minimize bare earth), climbers and perennial underplanting for trees and shrubs. Traditionally, gardens have been kept very tidy, which not only reduces habitat but also may make some pest problems worse. For example, conventional advice is to remove dead leaves from the ground if slugs and snails are a problem, as they supposedly find shelter there. However, leaf litter is also a favoured habitat for ground beetles, which eat slugs, as well as for such larger predators as frogs, toads and newts.

For the most part, gardeners can create gardens that look decorative *and* feed and house wildlife. The human eye delights in variety, and since nature also loves diversity, there is no contradiction there. Garden ponds are a particularly valuable way of increasing diversity, not just for land-dwelling wildlife to drink from, but also as additional habitat. A few wildlife-friendly garden features are not particularly ornamental, however, and might need to be hidden away; one of the best is the log-pile, a stack of decaying wood, which supports a wide range of invertebrates.

The growth in interest in gardening for wildlife has resulted in a flurry of products being developed and marketed, supposedly providing tailor-made habitats: hedgehog houses, bumblebee shelters, hibernation boxes for lacewing flies, and the like. While bird and bat boxes have been shown to work, clear evidence of whether many of these untested products actually help remains to be seen. More worryingly, they convey the wrong message: that by simply buying a product the gardener is in some way helping garden biodiversity, whereas the evidence is that what *really* helps is habitat and varied planting.

NATURAL-STYLE PLANTING TODAY

Many assume that natural-style planting is a new idea. Far from it! Its roots lie in the eighteenth-century English landscape tradition, when landowners in Britain tore out the geometrically organized hedges and trees of the Baroque era and replaced them with grassy banks, clumps of trees and sinuously bending lakes. The idea soon spread to the rest of Europe, and was taken up with greatest enthusiasm in Germany, where it was seen as symbolic of the Enlightenment and human progress.

Early in the twentieth century a number of landscape designers and writers about nature and gardens proposed adopting a style that either used native plants in preference to imported ones, and natural species as opposed to hybrids, or blended the features of natural vegetation with carefully chosen non-native species. In Britain, William Robinson (1838–1935) proposed 'naturalizing' garden plants among wild vegetation; the popularity today of growing daffodils in rough grass dates back to him. In the United States, Warren H. Manning (1860–1938) promoted a garden style that evoked natural habitats, as part of a movement that aimed at developing a distinctively American landscape style. In Germany, Willy Lange (1864–1941) wrote extensively about gardens that used native plants. Perhaps the most important figure, however, was the German nurseryman and writer Karl Foerster

Opposite, top The human desire to add water to a garden seems universal. A pond or stream is always a great wildlife resource, particularly when it is fringed with marginal planting, as in this garden by John Brookes.

Opposite, bottom, and left Diversity is key in wildlife-friendly plantings. In a vegetable garden, such flowering plants as these orange marigolds (*Calendula officinalis*; *opposite*) attract insect pollinators for crops. Unmown grass and slowly decaying wood are not the normal idea of a respectable garden, but both provide first-class wildlife habitats. Here (*left*), the wood not only has a function (a low barrier) but also looks decorative. Both images show Brockwell Park Community Greenhouses in south London.

(1874–1970), not because he promoted naturalistic planting as such, but because of the many herbaceous plants he introduced to cultivation; in particular, he made gardeners more aware of the value of groups that had not been used before, such as grasses.

A flurry of interest in looking to nature for garden inspiration began in the 1980s, largely growing out of the environmentalist movement. Foerster's promotion of grasses and perennials had laid the groundwork for research in Germany into planting combinations for public spaces that were low-maintenance, sustainable and wildlife-friendly. Today the country has far and away the largest number of truly inspirational naturalistic planting styles, mostly in public parks that originated as show events. Germany has also led the way in providing funding for research at universities and other institutions into sustainable planting with perennials. Fundamental to the German approach is an understanding of the ecological requirements of plants.

In the USA, the work of Wolfgang Oehme (who was born in Germany and heavily influenced by Foerster) and James van Sweden has brought into the public eye, and to great acclaim, a style of planting that relies heavily on herbaceous plants and grasses. While their work is only loosely naturalistic, it evokes the beauty of natural habitats, in particular the prairies, an environment dominated by grasses. Similarly inspired by natural habitats is Dutch designer Piet Oudolf, whose love of combining herbaceous plants with a strong sense of architecture has reconciled many to the idea that using perennials and grasses does not mean a garden must look wild. While Oudolf's work is not necessarily naturalistic or ecological as are the German parks plantings, it relies heavily on the intrinsic natural aesthetics of plants. Oudolf stresses the importance of gardeners and designers appreciating the structure of plants, their flower shapes, the arrangement of their stems and their winter appearance. Following in the Foerster tradition, Oudolf has done much to promote less familiar plant groups, such as umbellifers (Umbelliferae/Apiaceae), members of the parsley or carrot family. In Britain, such designers as Dan Pearson and Jinny Blom work with a wide range of perennials in a naturalistic style.

PLANTS FOR NATURAL-STYLE PLANTING

As we have seen, plants in a natural-style garden should maintain the proportions and style of their wild ancestors. The mix of plants is important, too. Gardeners have conventionally relied heavily on limited numbers of plant groups with prominent and colourful flowers. Those who wish to make wilder-style gardens need to cast their nets wider, or at least in a different direction, if they are to capture the essence of nature.

Grasses, and the distantly related but superficially very similar sedges (species of *Carex*) and wood rushes (species of *Luzula*), dominate many wild habitats — meadows, pasture, prairie, savannah — to the extent that they form a matrix into which other species have to fit as best they can. Including them in the garden is one of the most important ways of evoking a sense of the natural. The last decade of the twentieth century saw a great growth in interest in grasses, one result of which was the selection by nurseries of some very good garden-worthy varieties.

The daisy family (Compositae/Asteraceae) is one of the most widely distributed and numerous flowering perennials, particularly in North American prairie habitats. Many daisies have a long history in cultivation, but there are many more that are new or have not yet been evaluated for garden use. Natural-style gardeners will find that they make great use of them. Less important in North America, but a major element in many European landscapes, are the umbellifers; being

The Lurie garden in Chicago's Millennium Park, designed by Dutch designer Piet Oudolf, uses about one-third native species of the American Midwest to two-thirds conventional horticultural perennials. It is a good example of a nature-inspired public planting that is helping to show private gardeners just how much can be achieved with wild plants.

subtle in their colouring (most have cream flowers) they have historically been ignored by gardeners. Their structure, however, especially in the winter, is very strong, and for this reason they have recently found favour. Both umbellifers and grasses have seed heads that are a valuable winter food resource for birds.

Finally, the hardy geraniums need to be considered as important plants for the natural-style garden. Unlike the plant families just mentioned, the geraniums do not dominate any natural habitat. They are, however, immensely useful for the gardener, as they flower for months, are very easy to grow, and are excellent for suppressing weeds in parts of the garden where maintenance is difficult. They give colour from early summer, at a time when many larger perennials are still just neat mounds of leaves. One of the most valuable aspects is that they all, even modern nursery-bred hybrids, look natural, maintaining the proportions of their wild ancestors. They are ideal plants for the modern, nature-inspired garden.

An important part of natural-style gardening is finding plants that grow well in your conditions, and which you feel convey a sense of nature and wildness. This is not a style of gardening that follows a set of rules but one that involves developing an intuitive sense of what works in a particular place. Trial and error are a large part of this learning process: successful naturalistic gardeners are not afraid of making mistakes. This book aims at introducing gardeners to a style of working that engages with a sense of place, uses plants that suit the place and manages the plant community that develops when different species are combined.

Meadows

MEADOWS. LONG GRASS, SPANGLED WITH colourful wild flowers, waving in the breeze. For many of us the word 'meadow' conjures up one of the most desirable and romantic elements of both nature and today's wilder-style gardens. Meadows were once essential to farming, and although they are nowadays more likely to be an occasional anachronism or part of a nature reserve, they remain an essential part of our romantic image of the rural past. The garden meadow is a profound rejection of the more recent past, in particular the tradition of lawns and of mowing, a rejection of grass as simply a medium with which to create a flat green surface. A garden meadow shows that a garden does not simply involve controlling nature but also entering into a partnership with it. Its sometimes rough and tangled look rails against the conservatism and conformity of the lawn; it is the firmest statement of intent that a garden is not just about neatly trimmed beds and shaved grass.

Previous page In many country gardens there will already be some grassland. Its particular value is as a foreground to the surroundings. At Waltham Place garden in Berkshire, designed by Henk Gerritsen, a hedge is being established as a replacement for fencing. Much rough grassland can be made more interesting and biodiverse over the years through regular cutting and removal of the clippings. It is also possible to break up the surface and sow wild-flower seed to introduce new species.

Right, top A meadow created in a country garden by Jinny Blom. By blurring the boundaries between garden and surroundings, and between grass and borders, it helps the property to settle into and belong to its landscape.

Right, bottom Some of the best wild-flower meadow mixes are gathered from old-established fields, using adapted agricultural machinery. More conventionally, individual species are grown as field crops, so their seed can be made into mixes of varying content. Different mixes are recommended for various habitats, and for different parts of the same area. Pictured are Jane Lipington and Donald MacIntyre of Emorsgate Seeds in Somerset.

Opposite A traditional hay meadow on limestone, with a variety of spotted orchid (*Dactylorhiza fuchsii*), agrimony (*Agrimonia eupatoria*) and species of clover (*Trifolium*) and knapweed (*Centaurea*), the result of centuries of land management, chiefly cutting for hay.

Whereas a lawn always looks the same, a meadow is constantly changing. If a lawn looks different from the way it 'normally' looks, that is usually because there is a problem: it is drying out, becoming choked with moss or suffering a nutrient deficiency. A meadow, on the other hand, changes its colour and texture as it grows through the year – it feels dynamic and alive, with a personality, a will and a trajectory of its own.

It does not take much reflection to realize that meadow-making is more sustainable than lawn maintenance. Just think of all that pollution made by lawnmowers, and all the fuel used. A meadow is also much more wildlife-friendly; while a lawn supports little biodiversity in its short blades of grass, a meadow can be home to a rich variety of invertebrates, which in turn feed other valuable animals, especially birds.

Here, we need first of all to look at what meadows are, and at the different types, before discussing how they can be made and used in the garden. Key to understanding them is that, with the exception of mountain meadows (where only grasses and herbaceous plants can grow above the treeline), meadows are the result of human interaction with nature.

Many traditional farming systems encouraged the growth of grass by clearing trees and scrub. Farmers would cut the grass annually and store it dry as hay over

the winter in order to feed cattle or other livestock when there was not enough for them to eat outside. The distinction between meadow – grown for a grass crop – and pasture – which was regularly grazed by animals – is very important. No grazing animals would be allowed near a traditional meadow until after its midsummer cut, for they would trample and foul the crop. Although grass for hay-making was the objective of these traditional agricultural systems, a great many herbaceous flowering species grew alongside the grass species. Consequently, traditional meadows were a sea of wild flowers in the spring and early summer.

Modern agricultural systems aim to increase productivity by feeding the grass, either with (organic) nitrogen-rich manure or chemical fertilizers. Since grasses, and ryegrass in particular, are able to assimilate nitrogen faster and more effectively than nearly all wild-flower species, the result of intensification is the loss of wild flowers, and modern ryegrass-dominated fields can be less biodiverse than the average desert. There is a fundamentally important message here for the gardener: the more nitrogen in the soil, the better the grass will grow, and the fewer wild flowers there will be.

Opposite One of the bravest places for a wild-flower meadow is just outside the house. In this garden by John Brookes, knapweed (*Centaurea scabiosa*) makes a vibrant splash of colour. This and many other European wild-flower species are easiest to establish on shallow calcareous (chalky) soils. The few grass species that survive on such soils tend to be less vigorous, so there is less of a problem with long, rank growth.

Right, top One of the most effective ways of using wild-flower meadow is as a contrast to formality. In this Warwickshire garden by Dan Pearson, the meadow runs alongside a formal pool and mown lawn.

Right, bottom This is the country idyll that many imagine: livestock in natural-looking, fertile surroundings. The designer is Lesley Rosser. Long grass and wild flowers beneath fruit trees is a romantic combination, but it only works with mature trees, as grass will compete with the roots of younger ones.

Slower-growing wild-flower species are easily ousted by aggressive grass species. Most garden meadows aim for a proportion of grass to wild flower of about three to one; high fertility will shift the balance in favour of the grasses.

The balance of competition between grasses and wild flowers is dependent on fertility levels and the length of the growing season, a circumstance that helps to explain why some semi-natural environments have richer, more interesting and more beautiful wild-flower meadows than others. The best are in mountain areas, where, despite agricultural systems that use a lot of nitrogen-based feeding (in the form of manure), the short growing season ensures that grasses and wild flowers compete on a fairly equal footing. The worst are in well-watered lowlands on fertile soils in areas with a maritime climate, where the grass can grow for nearly 365 days of the year, excluding nearly all wild-flower species apart from the odd dock or thistle.

In much of Europe, the best wild flowers are to be found on limestone soils, which are drought-prone and

often infertile. Many of these environments are grazed, and are therefore technically pasture rather than meadow, but the key factor is that grass growth is limited by summer drought and low nitrogen levels. The result is that slower-growing but much more stress-tolerant wild-flower species have the opportunity to flourish. Such places are among the most magical of all landscapes: a short, fine turf full of brightly coloured wild flowers, or masses of blooms dominating thin grass between sun-bleached exposed rocks.

Botanists recognize major differences between the floras of these various types of meadow, in particular that the spartan conditions of dry limestone support many species not found elsewhere. For our purposes, however, many wild-flower species are to be found in a range of different habitats, and these adaptable generalists are particularly useful plants for the meadow gardener. Among them are the cranesbill geraniums, such as *Geranium pratense*, notable for its large blue flowers held well above the surrounding grass, and the mysterious maroon shades of its relative *Geranium phaeum*; the vivid purple-shot blue of tufted vetch (*Vicia cracca*) distributed liberally over the grasses by its sturdy climbing and scrambling stems; and the mauve–pink tufted heads of knapweeds (species of *Centaurea*).

A common feature of meadow flowers is early flowering. With a cut only a few weeks after midsummer's day, nothing that flowers later would have any chance of long-term survival in a traditional meadow. Another common feature is an ability to recover quickly from cutting and to grow another set of stems and leaves alongside the grasses. In some cases, especially if there are good late-summer rains, there may be repeat flowering, too. In garden management terms, this midsummer cut is very useful. Long grass and wild flowers look beautiful, but shortly after midsummer the grass begins to seed, and to look rank and untidy. As stems fall, the

Opposite, top The patchy appearance of this meadow by Jinny Blom is due to the growth of clover (species of *Trifolium*). Different wild-flower species are often able to share the same space because their roots are at different depths; grass roots tend to be shallow but most wild flowers go deeper, enabling them to stay greener for longer in droughts. Clovers, like most other members of the pea family, fix (assimilate) nitrogen in the soil, so contributing to soil fertility, which may also account for their vivid green.

Opposite, bottom Wild carrot (*Daucus carota*) is a common constituent of commercial wild-flower seed

mixes. However, it is a biennial and tends to die out in time, except on very poor soils. The presence of short-lived species in a seed mix has its uses, as they can help reduce weed and grass competition and so make space for slower-growing wild flowers. This planting is by Dan Pearson.

Left Ox-eye daisy (*Leucanthemum vulgare*) is a short-lived species that tends to dominate newly sown meadows, often spectacularly, as with this one by Jinny Blom. It is dependent on soil disturbance to provide places for new seedlings. As grasses establish, the daisies have less and less room to do this. Other, longer-lived plants will then take over.

meadow takes on a rumpled look, and even the most enthusiastic wild gardener will appreciate that it is well and truly over. Cutting tidies it up, and within a few weeks the surface is fresh with green new growth.

Some grassland habitats stay tidier for longer. The short turf of nutrient-poor limestone grassland or poor pasture habitats is dominated not by mat-forming grasses but by sedges, rushes and bunch grasses. Such habitats are a useful model for garden meadows on low-fertility soils. As well as looking good for longer, they may contain wild-flower species that flower in late summer, such as the startling yellow daisies of common fleabane (*Pulicaria dysenterica*) or devil's bit scabious (*Succisa pratensis*), which creates a blue haze.

In the garden, the word 'meadow' is best restricted to grass-dominated plantings that are cut at least once a year. There is clearly a gradation, starting off with a lawn that may be cut every week in the summer, through grass with a regime of cutting every few weeks, to rough grass meadow, which may be cut only annually. Just beyond the lawn on this spectrum is the 'mini-meadow', essentially a lawn that contains some of the common lawn 'weeds', such low-growing plants as daisies (*Bellis perennis*) and self-heal (*Prunella vulgaris*). This habitat makes a particularly good place for small, early-flowering plants, such as cowslips (*Primula veris*) or bulbs.

Growing daffodils (species of *Narcissus*) in grass is a long-established practice, as they make much more rapid growth than grass does at the end of the winter. Other bulbs, such as snowdrops (species of *Galanthus*) and crocuses, may also be successful in the weaker grass of lightly shaded areas. Once they have flowered, the grass must not be cut until the bulbs' foliage has died down, as otherwise they will not be able to store away enough nutrients to flower the next year. Since daffodil foliage may hang around for months, growing steadily less attractive, it makes good sense to make the most of the resulting 'meadow by default' and include some early-blooming wild flowers. For those new to the idea of the meadow or cautious about it, 'naturalizing' daffodils and other robust bulbs in grass is a good way to start.

A fundamental difference between meadow gardening and conventional gardening is that in the latter we cultivate plants as individuals, but in the meadow every plant is treated the same way. Just as a lawn is composed of thousands of individual grass plants that all get the same treatment – all being mown or fertilized together – so is a meadow. This is known as 'extensive' management, in contrast to the 'intensive' management of conventional border plantings. This means that we have very little direct control over the composition of a meadow. Over time – indeed from year to year – the species composition can change. This is one of the great joys of meadow gardening: that it is never the same; that it can look quite different from one year to the next, as species ebb and flow according to the weather or the internal dynamic of the plant community. Different management regimes, chiefly changing cutting times and frequencies, are among the tools gardeners have to try to shift the species composition one way or another (see pages 180–81).

One particularly interesting aspect of the extensive management of meadows is the spontaneous appearance of plant species, apparently from nowhere. The seed of a surprising number of wild-flower species is always drifting around, but will never grow into an adult plant if conditions are not right. People who have managed

At his own weekend home, the leading US landscape architect James van Sweden has chosen bold clumps of grasses (*Panicum virgatum*) to segue into the grasses of the surrounding semi-natural landscape.

a meadow for a number of years will report a sense of surprise and wonder at the arrival of plant species that they may never have seen locally. Orchids, in particular, tend to appear by surprise, but then their seed is extraordinarily small and produced in prodigious quantities. The arrival of such spontaneous additions is a sign that you have created a welcoming environment, that what you have made is not fixed by the number of species in the original seed packet, but is a living and ever-changing entity that could continue to increase in diversity through natural processes for many years.

Another aspect of extensive management is the way a meadow develops different plant combinations in different areas. Usually when a meadow is made, one seed mix is scattered over the whole area, unless conditions are so clearly varied in different parts of the site that separate mixes are used (for wet or dry soil conditions, for example). Inevitably, though, there will be small differences in soil moisture, nutrient content or aspect from one area to another, and over time the mix of species will begin to reflect this. The result will be a complex patchwork, with some species more common in some areas of the meadow than others. This is especially noticeable with plants that form extensive clumps, such as clovers (species of *Trifolium*).

We tend to think of meadows as relatively large-scale features, or most appropriate in country gardens. They are especially appreciated as a foreground to rural

Above A path mown through long grass is one of the most romantic of all garden features. This is the Fox Garden by Julie Toll; the predominant flower here is ox-eye daisy, *Leucanthemum vulgare*.

Opposite In a garden by Jinny Blom, a strip of rough grass is studded with a number of vigorous perennials, including two species of scabious – *Knautia macedonica* and *K. arvensis* – and white *Centranthus ruber* 'Albus'. There are also foxgloves, *Digitalis purpurea*.

Left, top A number of dry-habitat plants grown as a border planting, which could be a striking accompaniment to a dry meadow. In this Warwickshire garden by Dan Pearson, the tall spikes are *Eremurus × isabellinus* 'Cleopatra', the silver is *Eryngium giganteum* and the purple is *Salvia nemorosa*, which can be grown alongside grasses in meadows.

Left, bottom More typical of very dry Mediterranean-climate regions are bunch grasses and grey-leaved dwarf shrubs. In the Valentine Garden in Santa Barbara, California, by Isabelle Greene, a *Pennisetum* grass grows alongside silvery artemisias. Such plants are also very useful for dry situations in other climate zones.

Opposite Thymes are a natural component of meadows on dry, calcareous soils. At Home Farm in Northamptonshire, Dan Pearson has used them to dramatic effect to create a 'thyme meadow'. In the top view, their colour has been picked out in the border by *Salvia verticillata* 'Purple Rain'. The use of creeping thymes in this way is most likely to succeed on soils that are so dry that normal grass growth is impeded.

views, providing a gentle transition between tame garden and the wilder landscape beyond. There is no reason, however, why they cannot play a positive part in small or urban gardens, too. Meadows can be small: even just a square metre or yard. Such dwarf meadows are best developed as part of a more conventional lawn, as surrounding short grass will help to contextualize the long grass and wild flowers. Dwarf meadows often work best as strips or elongated shapes. There are two provisos, though. One is that the smaller the meadow, the better it will look with shorter grass and wild-flower species; rain-soaked and wind-blown long grass does not look good close up. The other is that such features are often most successful when they are treated as seasonal, being allowed to grow for the spring and early summer, as a way of enjoying fresh meadow flowers at their best, but being kept cut relatively short for the period after midsummer.

Meadows can be used simply as an alternative to lawn, but in most gardens it is practicable to develop them as a replacement for only a proportion of the lawn. Ensuring that meadows fit in with the layout and look of the rest of the garden is important, and there are a number of ways of doing it. Given that in most gardens that include a wild area, there is a clear gradation from a 'tidy' area near the house to a 'wilder' area further away, it makes sense to have mown lawn nearer the house, and the meadow further back. Narrow paths mown through meadow, or just long grass, make for one of the most romantic 'special effects' in gardening. Unless a path is straight, it is visible for only a short distance ahead, so one's further exploration becomes inherently a mystery. Paths are an invitation to plunge in, tread the unknown, and be surrounded and seduced by waving, shimmering grasses.

A pattern of mowing that leaves geometric meadow patches can also be highly effective, and makes it very clear that the meadow is intentional. The mowing pattern

can even be changed every year, so that it becomes a design element in itself. Regular closer or more frequent mowing of some areas will result in a gradation of grass at various heights, with the advantage that different wild-flower and grass floras will develop in each area. This will be reflected in different invertebrate populations.

It may be a paradox to gardeners, who are used to thinking of fertility and moisture as good, that poor and dry soils often support the most diverse wild-flower floras. It is a fundamental fact of plant ecology, though, that with lower levels of food and water there is more space for more species; difficult growing conditions make for small plants, which leave each other more room, while rich, moist habitats fuel lush and vigorous growth, resulting in a 'fight to the finish' and a restricted number of species. Very dry meadow habitats can be particularly interesting and visually exciting. For gardeners with light sandy soils, or who experience frequent droughts, such places offer hope, inspiration and a source of knowledge.

Particularly inspiring are the dry meadows of central Europe, where the climate exposes plants to cold winters and hot, dry summers. Further east is the steppe, the great grasslands of central Asia. The steppe has provided us with some good garden plants, including *Perovskia atriplicifolia* (Russian sage), whose haze of blue-violet flowers is at its best in late summer, and the foxtail lilies (*Eremurus*), bulbs with majestic spires of small flowers in

In all three of these gardens by Piet Oudolf, the grass used is *Deschampsia cespitosa*, a common northern European species of infertile soils. In nature it rarely forms 'meadows' like this, but in the garden it can be highly effective, with its characteristic haze of flowers appearing in early summer, turning to seed heads (shown here), which last until late autumn. Flowering perennials can be interspersed for a dramatic contrast. The species is inclined to be short-lived, but will self-sow. Other species are suitable for creating this effect, notably the drought-tolerant *Sporobolus heterolepis*. The space above left was designed by Piet Boon; the sculptor is Bart van Hoek.

early summer. Many steppe plants do not just look good when they flower, but also have seed heads with sculptural qualities that contribute to the garden for a long time after the flowers have finished.

There is an overlap between the flora of the steppe and that of the Mediterranean. Grasses in the genus *Stipa*, for example, can be found in both regions. The one best known by gardeners is *Stipa gigantea*, with its clump of evergreen leaves and tall heads of oat-like panicles that are never still unless the air is absolutely calm. This grass illustrates a key difference between two groups of grasses, which is very important to understand. The meadow grasses of humid climates in Europe tend to run, so that they form turf (or sod); this is made great use of in lawns, where an interpenetrated mat of grass is essential. Grasses of other regions and climates form tight clumps – the so-called 'bunch grasses'. Their appearance is very different, as it is usually possible to discern each individual clump.

Bunch grasses can be very useful in the garden for providing striking visual effects, which could be described as 'stylized meadow': either grouping plants to create strikingly contemporary blocks of grass, or mixing in a limited number of strongly structural flowering perennials. Such 'bunch-grass meadows' are perhaps the best solution for North American gardeners, whose landscape has few naturally sod-forming grasses. The word 'meadow' has, in any case, been somewhat misinterpreted in North America. Hay-making was not a part of land management before the European settlement, although prairie burning was (see page 48), so there are no true native grass 'meadows' in North America. Introduced European sod-forming grasses can be used to create meadows, however, with both introduced and native wild flowers; unfortunately, this has been little researched so far. Shorter prairie species can also be used to create attractive meadow-like

features. Commercially, however, meadow seed mixes have been promoted, largely containing annuals or short-lived perennials. The result is usually a one-year spectacular followed by a decline in interest, leading to misunderstanding and disillusionment.

Plantings based on such bunch grasses as prairie dropseed (*Sporobolus heterolepis*) or the European *Deschampsia cespitosa* are undeniably spectacular and have a long season of interest. Many species that can be used are relatively drought-tolerant, short-grass prairie plants or their European equivalent, steppe grasses. Such plantings are an obvious solution for gardeners in places where a dry season is normal or likely, whether this is a sizeable area in a dry region or a small patch of poor, dry soil in a moist region.

Superficially very similar to bunch grasses are the many sedges (species of *Carex*), typically plants of poor

Right, top Stipa tenuissima is a striking, small bunch grass with a remarkably long season, wonderfully effective if scattered among perennials of a similar size, as here by Henk Gerritsen at Waltham Place in Berkshire. It is short-lived but usually re-sows.

Right, bottom Molinia caerulea, seen here at Bury Court in Hampshire, by Piet Oudolf, is a bunch grass of acidic soils in northern Europe, ideal for making rather formal, stylized meadow effects. Several cultivars are now available, varying considerably in height.

Opposite, left Deschampsia cespitosa grass used here by Dan Pearson with yellow *Rudbeckia fulgida* is intended as an artistic evocation of a meadow, with surrounding shrubs representing the hedges of the surrounding landscape.

Opposite, top right Any grass tends to remind us of the wild. In this planting at Sticky Wicket in Dorset, the short-lived but usually self-seeding wild barley *Hordeum jubatum* displays its highly distinctive heads among *Salvia sclarea* var. *turkestanica* and the globes of ornamental onions (species of *Allium*).

Opposite, bottom right Stipa gigantea is far too big, at nearly 2 m (6 ft), to be a meadow grass, but it evokes wild grasslands extremely well through its vast panicles of oat-like heads, which move constantly in the slightest breeze. It comes from the Mediterranean but is perfectly hardy, and grown en masse makes a good weed-suppressant. This garden in Devon is by Karena Batstone.

soils and often cold, exposed habitats. Mass plantings of sedges, which have the advantage for gardeners of being evergreen, and frequently have attractive bronze foliage, are a good design solution for poor soils in cold areas. Where they are interspersed with appropriate wild flowers or such dwarf shrubs as heathers (*Calluna vulgaris* and species of *Erica*), the results can be attractive and low-maintenance.

Opposite A gate makes a transition between the ordered garden and a wilder area beyond. Borders of perennials and meadow can echo each other, especially if some species manage a cross-over. This image and that above show a garden by Jinny Blom.

Above Rough grass is a sensible, low-maintenance and sustainable alternative to mowing in situations where a tidy look is not needed. It also looks so much more appropriate next to an informal hedge and trees than mown grass does.

Prairies and Borders

S TRETCHING ACROSS VAST EXPANSES OF THE
American Midwest, the prairie was once one
of the world's greatest wild-flower spectacles, a
seemingly endless sea of grasses sparkling with
an incredible variety of flowers. It consisted of a range
of different habitats and plant communities, the common
factor being the dominance of a number of species of
grass. The grasses and wild flowers grew to well above
head height, and often the only way to see ahead was
from horseback. The prairie has now been almost
entirely cleared for agriculture.

To the north and east, the prairie gave way to
savannah and then forest; to the west, a community
of shorter grasses (short-grass prairie; see page 42)
gradually gave way to sagebrush and desert. The
intermingling of savannah and grassland formed a
particularly complex boundary, and it is now known that
its character was largely defined by the habit of Native
American people of deliberately creating fires in order to
provide more land for buffalo and game (among several
possible reasons). Savannah is itself a complex habitat, an
ever-changing tapestry of patches of trees surrounded by
grass, grassy glades in woodland, single trees scattered
over grassland, and every other conceivable combination
of tree and grass.

The American prairie seems a long way from the
herbaceous border of the English garden tradition. Yet
many of the herbaceous plants at the core of the English
border are of prairie origin, introduced into cultivation
from North America from the eighteenth century
onwards: Michaelmas daisies (*Aster novi-belgii* hybrids)
and other species of aster, solidago (goldenrod), phlox,
monarda and many more. In its well-manicured and
ordered golden age, the early twentieth century, the
English border's main season in late summer and
early autumn reflected the high point of floral interest
in the prairie.

Traditional border plants were selected and hybridized for the impact of their flowers, but top-heavy flower heads weakened stems, so they needed to be staked. Many varieties needed frequent division to stay healthy too. The result was that herbaceous plants acquired a reputation for being labour-intensive. Since the 1970s, however, many more have been introduced into cultivation, or at least popularized, that are much less demanding in their requirements, and with a natural proportion and elegance. They have been joined by many earlier-flowering plants, disregarded by previous generations of gardeners, in particular the geraniums (the true geraniums, as opposed to the half-hardy pelargoniums popularly known by this name). Perhaps most radical has been the popularization of many species of ornamental grasses – a plant family almost totally ignored in the past. It is this coming together of a wide range of grasses and flowering perennials that has made

Pages 46–47 This photograph of the Prairie Garden at Chicago Botanic Garden gives a clear idea of the complexity of prairie. Note the wide range of colours and textures: there are many different combinations of plants, in each of which one species tends to dominate. These combinations reflect subtle changes in many factors: moisture availability, soil chemistry, history of disturbance, or the chance arrival of strongly spreading species. When an artificial prairie is sown, the appearance will at first be more uniform, but the component species will gradually rearrange themselves, and more will arrive on the wind in years to come.

Opposite Blue *Aster laevis*, white *A. pilosus* and yellow *Solidago canadensis* all flower in late summer in a habitat restored by Tom Vanderpoel and Citizens for Conservation, Illinois. Many later-flowering prairie perennials are yellow, with blue or purple the next most common. These complementary colours are often seen together in open habitats in eastern North America at that time of year. The implication for domestic gardeners is clear: here is a good garden combination for the end of the summer.

Above Even at the very end of the flowering year the prairie is visually interesting, with seed heads silhouetted against foliage. As the leaves begin to die they will change to fawns and browns. This is by Neil Diboll, in Wisconsin.

herbaceous planting such a fast-moving and rapidly
developing field. The American prairie is the chief
natural inspiration behind the modern nature-inspired
border. Indeed, modern perennial and grass planting
is sometimes referred to as 'prairie planting', but this is
a very inaccurate description if no prairie species are
actually included.

Just as with a wild-flower meadow, it is important
to stress the difference between true prairie habitat and a
garden planting designed to evoke the wild habitat. True
prairies and meadows contain plants that are far more
densely packed than any designed border. This density
gives them a resilience that designed borders lack: leave
a meadow or prairie unmanaged for a few years and it
will still have its essential character and species mix, but
leave a border for a few years and it will appear radically
different, as uninvited species from the wild and the
most vigorously spreading border components will
occupy all bare ground between the original plants.
True prairie is a dynamic plant community, with its own
rules and trajectory, very poorly understood even by
ecologists. A prairie- or meadow-inspired border in the
garden may look very different from the conventional
herbaceous border, but is still similar in management
terms; it needs looking after if it is to retain its looks.
Here, I will briefly consider prairie-making, but
concentrate on the modern herbaceous border.

Prairie, like meadow, is composed of a matrix
of grasses (and sometimes sedges), with flowering
perennials (known as forbs) as the minority element.
Mature, established prairie is dominated very clearly
by grasses, of which one species, *Andropogon gerardii*,
dominates the tall-grass prairie of the moister western
belt. Younger prairie (that which has established more
recently on bare ground or on land cleared of trees)
has a more varied flora and includes far more flowering
plants, in particular goldenrods and asters. These

Opposite At Dan Pearson's garden at Home Farm in Northamptonshire, a scarlet day lily (*Hemerocallis*) is set off by the fawn shades of *Stipa gigantea*. This grass is invaluable: big enough to create impact, but with such sparse stems, flowers and seed heads that, in small quantities, it is 'transparent', and so not visually dominating.

Right, top Grasses (this is a species of *Stipa*) bring a real sense of the wild and the untamed to this double border at Sticky Wicket in Dorset. The white flowers are *Achillea millefolium*, useful for its long summer flowering season. Such a wild planting is a highly effective and appropriate complement to the rustic-style summerhouse.

Right, bottom Three of the most widely grown species of grass provide an effective backdrop to *Rudbeckia fulgida* in a garden by Dan Pearson in Warwickshire. The grass at the rear is *Calamagrostis × acutifolia* 'Karl Foerster', a good European alternative to American prairie grasses, invaluable for its long season of strongly vertical display. In the middle is *Deschampsia cespitosa*, which has a somewhat shorter season (midsummer to autumn). On the left is *Stipa gigantea*, illustrating this grass's special quality – its transparency.

plants tend to colonize strongly, but over time are slowly displaced by grasses and, to some extent, by members of the legume family. These last two groups of plants develop slowly but build up immense root systems with time, allowing them to dominate the ground and persist over many years.

Prairies, like wild-flower meadows, can be made by sowing a seed mix on to prepared soil (see pages 180–81). The seed mix is designed to give a grass-to-forb mix of about three to one – the same as a meadow. Seed mixes are available for different soils and for different moisture regimes, but can also be tailored for height, and even for colour. Just as with meadows, their appearance in the first few years will be dominated by those species that establish quickly but die out after a few years, the large-flowered and deservedly popular *Echinacea purpurea* and the pale yellow-flowered *Ratibida pinnata* among them. With time an equilibrium will be established, but the plant community will never stay exactly the same from year to year.

The modern, natural-style perennial border may take many forms. It will never be mistaken for a true prairie or any other wild or semi-wild habitat, but its plants will be much closer to their wild ancestors than those to be found in the stiff and regimented borders of the past. In many cases they will be genetically identical to the same species growing in the wild; in others the cultivated plants will be a superior selection made from wild-collected material. Even among the hybrids and the results of deliberate breeding, the proportion of flower to

Left Several aster and solidago species provide a naturalistic pond border in a planting by Tom Vanderpoel and Citizens for Conservation, Illinois. Dense vegetation beside water provides cover and shelter for wildlife, and can act as a barrier, preventing a fall into the water.

Opposite The silver–grey evergreen foliage of *Phlomis italica* provides a good contrast with the autumnal shades of grasses and perennials. This planting is by Isabelle van Groeningen and Gabriella Pape in their Oxfordshire garden.

Right, top This herbaceous scheme by Piet Oudolf at Bury Court in Surrey, seen in late summer, combines conventional planting (using a backdrop) with an open area, within the context of a relatively architectural garden design. The plant in the lower left is *Persicaria amplexicaulis*; behind it is *Monarda* 'Fishes'. On the right is pale-pink *Lythrum salicaria* 'Blush', and to the left of this is *Geranium wlassovianum*.

Right, bottom Conventional borders have a backdrop, but if there is only a narrow space between the backdrop and any other boundary, such as this path, the result can be problematic, especially if a thirsty hedge is involved. The grass in this midsummer border in Piet Oudolf's own garden at Hummelo, The Netherlands, is *Deschampsia cespitosa*, which has rather more tolerance of growing beneath or around trees than most grasses. The pink–red heads are *Monarda* 'Balance'. At the back is *Angelica gigas*, a striking umbellifer with unusual maroon flower heads. Like most umbellifers it is biennial, but unlike most it does not reliably self-sow, making it necessary for gardeners to collect seed and sow it themselves in order to maintain stock of the plant.

leaf and stem will be very similar to that found among wild plants.

Grasses have an important role in the modern nature-inspired border. The more there are in proportion to other elements, especially if they are multiple individuals of the same species, the more naturalistic the border will look. And the presence of grasses in the modern border raises an interesting point about how we look at perennial-dominated plantings.

Traditional borders tend to be linear, with a backdrop of a hedge, fence or wall, or take the form of island beds, with taller plants in the middle and shorter ones around the outside. This means that plants tend to be seen lit from the front, a circumstance that is fine for most flowers, but not very flattering to grass flowers or their seed heads. On the other hand, grasses can often be magically transformed by being lit from the back, their heads sparkling in the sunlight or showing colours that are all but invisible when lit from the front. Backlighting or sidelighting is particularly important in the autumn and winter, when colours are limited to browns and fawns. These colours can seem dull, but when struck by the low-angled, warm colours of early-morning or evening winter sunlight, dead leaves and stems positively glow. The lesson is that modern borders need to break away from the traditional format and let the light in.

The herbaceous border of the past relied on herbaceous perennials, of course, but also, to some extent, on bulbs and annuals. Later developments produced the

A wilder take on the border, by Jinny Blom. The foaming yellow flowers are *Alchemilla mollis*, a well-established and very robust border plant. The white is *Valeriana officinalis*, a wetland perennial that in this border has begun to self-sow. Breaking with the 'tallest at the back' tradition, this spontaneous scattering creates a very wild effect. This is a cool and sophisticated combination, but what is notable about the flower colours of both these plants is that they combine well with many others.

'mixed border', with a greater role for shrubs, climbers and even small trees. The result was in some ways more naturalistic, as the combination of woody plants with perennials is very similar to the combination of shrubs, climbers and perennials found in many woodland-edge or hedgerow habitats. Because of the presence of woody plants, however, the mixed border was still suited to the 'tallest at the back, shortest at the front' plan, which still worked against using grasses.

Grasses work best combined with a minimum of woody plants, partly because they appreciate high levels of all-round light, and partly because they look best lit from the back as well as from the front. The meadow or the prairie, then, is the best natural model and inspiration for plantings that use grasses. Given that most gardeners want flowers above all else, herbaceous perennials will continue to dominate the border, but shorter-lived plants, such as annuals and biennials, will also have a role to play. Many are very colourful and some, biennials in particular, have striking seed heads, which are useful for winter interest. They are also important for introducing an essential element of spontaneity impossible for mere humans to achieve.

Opposite This very good, colourful example of the open border style is by Piet Oudolf at RHS Wisley, Surrey. Deep pink *Stachys officinalis* and its paler form 'Rosea' are combined with several forms of *Echinacea purpurea* and interwoven with clumps of *Molinia caerulea* subsp. *arundinacea*. There are also monarda hybrids at the rear.

Above The planting in this garden (Piet Oudolf's own, at Hummelo, The Netherlands) combines the conventional (a hedge acts as backdrop to the left) and the contemporary open border styles. A path encourages walking between the plants, so that they can be experienced more intimately than in a conventional border. In the right foreground is *Saponaria* × *lempergii* 'Max Frei'; left is *Stachys byzantina*. The tall plant at back right is *Eupatorium purpureum*, a species so tall (generally around 2 m/6 ft) that in most gardens it really does work best at the back of the border.

Many biennials and some annuals are very good at leaving behind just enough seedlings to provide some plants the following year, but in places *they* have chosen – hence the spontaneity. Among the biennials good for this are mulleins (species of *Verbascum*) – tall, usually with yellow-flowered spikes – and foxgloves (species of *Digitalis*). The same applies to many short-lived perennials: aquilegias are just one example of many that are invaluable for scattering themselves around, but usually without overdoing it.

The woody plants that combine best with grasses and perennials are the ones that are hardly woody at all: such sub-shrubs as lavender and cistus. Their low profile does not get in the way of the light, their hummocky shapes are a gentle contrast with the upright habit of many perennials, and their evergreen nature is a real boon during the winter months. Most are plants of dry or exposed habitats, although in fact they will generally survive and prosper anywhere with plenty of light and a well-drained soil.

Having established that perennial and grass combinations work best with few woody plants and without a backdrop, there remains the question of how to design the nature-inspired border. Much depends on the size and shape of the garden, of course. Since many gardens consist of large areas of lawn, the obvious question to ask is: Do you really want so much lawn? If you like flowers and plants and gardening, why maintain large areas of lawn? Lawns can be very useful – for sunbathing, children's play, parties and other activities – but if they are not actually needed, the next question to ask is whether they serve any kind of aesthetic function. They provide a good foreground to plantings of all kinds, and also give a Taoist sense of emptiness in the garden. What may seem a radical idea to some, that of digging up the lawn and planting up the area, makes perfect sense to anyone who either likes growing plants, especially

perennials, or is interested in creating wildlife habitat; apart from worms and grubs to feed some varieties of birds, lawns are not noted for their biodiversity.

What form the planted-up alternative to a lawn takes is a matter of taste. One happy idea is to create a series of narrow paths winding through really tall plants. The experience of walking along such paths captures just a little of the sense of walking through the prairie; of being among perennials and grasses at, or even above, head height; of experiencing a sense of awe and wonder. Of course, such height is maintained for only a few months, as, once cut down in the winter, such plantings will be reduced to ground level for several months.

Opposite, top A path sweeps through perennials and grasses in late summer at Broughton Hall in Yorkshire. Even this fairly broad path soon disappears behind planting, begging the question about where it goes next. Creating such mysteries is recognized as being at the core of garden design. This scheme, by Dan Pearson, features large blocks of plants, creating a dramatic effect but also simple to maintain. The grass is *Calamagrostis* × *acutifolia* 'Karl Foerster', the scarlet flowers *Persicaria amplexicaulis*, the pale pink *Veronicastrum virginicum* f. *roseum* and the fading flowers along the path by the seat *Salvia verticillata* 'Purple Rain'.

Opposite, bottom Late summer is when many North American prairie species are at their best. In this planting by Neil Diboll, mauve *Aster laevis* and white *A. ptarmicoides* combine with yellow *Rudbeckia triloba* to create a classic late-season mix. The rudbeckia is a short-lived perennial, with a lifespan of between three and five years, but it often self-sows. The reddish grass is *Schizachyrium scoparium*.

Above A dramatic midsummer example of how a formal garden has been transformed by new planting, superimposing a modern scheme on to a 1920s layout at Waltham Place, Berkshire. Areas of open border have been created, partly planted, partly gravelled, in Henk Gerritsen's design. The grass *Calamagrostis* × *acutifolia* 'Karl Foerster' is used as a theme plant, developing a strong sense of rhythm. The large-growing but non-spreading knotweed *Aconogonon* 'Johanniswolke' forms several clumps of fading white.

Such a change in magnitude over the course of a year creates a great sense of the change and dynamism of the seasons.

Another idea, if you do not find the concept of perennials above head height an attractive one, is to maintain the open feel of the garden, restricting plant height to below eye level. This makes it possible to look out over plants, to appreciate a complex tapestry of colour and texture. The occasional taller species can be added for extra interest: particularly useful here are those plants with a transparent quality, so that what is behind them is seen through a haze of stem and flower. Good examples are the grass *Stipa gigantea*, the purple-flowered *Verbena bonariensis* and all the larger thalictrums.

Modern borders that involve planting across space, and liberating the border from being only a border, are about creating spectacles and perspectives radically

Opposite An advantage of the open border style is the sense it creates that the planting covers much more ground than is actually the case. In this late-summer planting by Piet Oudolf at Bury Court, Surrey, the white *Actaea simplex* 'Prichard's Giant' creates statuesque clumps, which bring light to a scene otherwise dominated by the first signs of autumnal decay. The dark, rounded seed heads are *Angelica gigas*, and the bold leaves in the foreground belong to *Darmera peltata*. It and the actaea indicate a moist soil. The fresh green is the sedge *Carex muskingumensis*.

Right, top *Calamagrostis* × *acutifolia* 'Karl Foerster' is an effective mock prairie grass in this Warwickshire garden by Dan Pearson. It is remarkable for its long season, from early summer,

when it flowers, to late winter, when it must be cut down to make way for new growth. During that time it almost invariably stands well, coping with even hurricane-force winds. Only growing in less than full sunlight will weaken its resilient stems.

Right, bottom A big planting of bold perennials and grasses can look remarkably good in misty weather. Here, in late summer, is silver *Miscanthus sinensis* with *Panicum virgatum* (just beginning to show its capacity to develop some of the best autumn colour to be found among the grasses). The yellow is *Achillea filipendulina*, here putting on a second show (its usual season is early summer), and the red bobbles are *Sanguisorba tenuifolia*, a useful 'transparent' plant. The garden is by Cleve West, in Normandy.

different from the conventional. 'Open borders' is a good name for them, as it conveys a sense of freedom as well as being descriptive. Although they may be far removed from meadows and prairies in terms of ecology or composition, it is these great wild and natural open spaces that have provided much of the inspiration.

How, then, should the open border be laid out, and how should plants be selected and arranged? Simply ploughing up the lawn and planting right across it may seem disorientating at first. A good way to see how the space will work is to think about how it might be accessed. Paths are needed for maintenance and so that we can enjoy being at close quarters with the plants. As a general rule, 3 m (10 ft) of planting between paths is about as far as most of us would regard as being practicable. Many might prefer 2 m (6 ft).

At the very simplest level, an open border can be created by simply extending a conventional border, letting it flow outwards, away from its backdrop. For those new to the concept this is perhaps the best way to start. A curving path can be used between the original border and the new extension.

If relatively narrow paths follow gently winding courses they soon disappear from view behind planting, at least once growth has begun in the spring. The result is an illusion that the area of planting is a solid mass, whereas in fact it may be riven by a network of paths. The importance of this illusion cannot be underestimated. In order for this design device to work, paths must be as invisible as possible from the main viewpoint from which the planting is to be seen, and, as much as is practical, from the entry point to the path, too. Paths also need to be narrow, as the narrower they are the more readily they will disappear from view. However, very narrow paths (around 50 cm/20 in) are only sensible if the vegetation of the new border is to be relatively low, say 60 cm (2 ft) or less; taller plants may

flop over, especially in the rain, resulting in anyone navigating the network getting soaking wet. Paths of about 1 m (3 ft) work well enough, although some support, or regular cutting back, for any plants flopping over the edge may be necessary.

A new open border waiting to be planted may seem a somewhat intimidating prospect. How do you begin? Structural plants that last a long time are probably the best starting point; think of them in terms of the rhythm in a piece of music. Grasses or perennials that flower relatively early but maintain structure for a long time afterwards, such as *Veronicastrum virginicum*, are useful for this purpose. Such plants need to be repeated through the planting: it is this repetition of key plants that gives an open border a sense of coherence and a visual unity. An open area enthusiastically planted with lots of different species will all too easily look a mess, even more so than a conventional linear border. Once this basic coherence is achieved, any number of single individuals of different varieties can be planted.

One way of organizing the basic elements of an open border is to think in terms of 'theme plants', the long-season structural plants suggested above being the most important category. Theme plants provide a sense of order, coherence and rhythm. Each season, or even each month of the growing season, can have some theme plants, whose presence pulls the whole planting together. Bulbs are ideal for this in the spring, especially as they

Autumn colour is generally associated with trees, but many herbaceous plants and grasses have rich colours, too. They need to be correctly placed so that they can be illuminated by low-angled light, especially at the beginning or end of the day, when the proportion of red and yellow light is at its highest. In the foreground here at Isabelle van Groeningen and Gabriella Pape's Oxfordshire garden is a *Sedum spectabile* variety, a member of a late-flowering group of plants much sought after by butterflies; to the right is the grass *Molinia caerulea* subsp. *arundinacea*; below it is a whole range of colours on a geranium species.

are so easily scattered in an existing planting. Later theme plants need to have a number of characteristics: they must be reliable, be something you know thrives in your garden, have at least several weeks of flowering, and preferably combine colour with good form.

In considering theme plants, it will help you to develop a strong design if you think of them as defining the look for the time they are performing. Each season's colour scheme or character can be set by the theme plant. For example *Echinacea purpurea*, with its two months of big pink daisies, makes a reliable theme plant for mid- to late summer, in terms of both colour and structure. Other plants, with less structure or impact, can be added to complement it, such as monardas or *Stachys officinalis* and its cultivars, with flowers in pinks, mauves and purples.

In the most successful open borders, the plants appear to be scattered at random. It is in fact possible to create very successful plantings that *are* completely haphazard, but in most plantings this is more apparent than real. At first sight the wild flowers in a meadow may appear to be at random, but nature never is. Plants always grow somewhere for a reason: the soil may suit some species better in some places than others, resulting in different concentrations of the component species of a meadow in different areas; or the seeding strategy of the plant may result in varying distribution patterns. The most natural-looking plantings are often those that have been laid out by someone with an intuitive feel for the way plants are distributed in nature (see page 20). There are greater or lesser concentrations of particular species, and in particular there is often a drift of one species, but

Above and opposite Silhouettes are important in the autumn and winter (*above*). Taller perennials with dark remains, such as this achillea, are impressive either against the sky or against distant lighter plants, such as grasses. Another excellent autumn effect is the contrast between dark colours in well-defined shapes and pale colours in soft, ill-defined shapes (*opposite*). The seed heads of *Veronicastrum virginicum* dominate the foreground, and the flowers of *Aster lateriflorus* the background. Grasses provide the pale straw tones and soft textures. Both photographs show Isabelle van Groeningen and Gabriella Pape's own garden in Oxfordshire.

with 'outliers', or individuals scattered apart from the main group. Above all, the intermingling of different varieties is crucial to the natural look of the open border.

The height of interest in both the prairie and the traditional herbaceous border is late summer to autumn. In many ways this is true for the modern nature-inspired border, too. Provided the summers are not dry, there are definite advantages in having borders that are at their best later rather than earlier in the growing season. Many plants tend to look untidy after flowering, whereas before flowering they look neat, lush and full of promise, so there is an obvious advantage in prolonging that state. In addition, many early-flowering plants (in full flower at or before midsummer's day) do not have strong structures, so they will look untidy after flowering; late-summer- and autumn-flowering perennials, however, are more likely to be upright-growing and so have better post-flowering structure. Some of the most successful designers of borders use early- and late-blooming perennials in a ratio of around one to three.

This is not a hard-and-fast rule. *Veronicastrum virginicum*, with its strongly upright stems, is an example of a perennial that flowers relatively early (around midsummer) but looks upright and respectable for many months afterwards. Aquilegias and thalictrums (late spring to early summer) turn to slim and moderately interesting seed heads. Much early border interest does depend, though, on the hardy geraniums. More than anything else, it is these plants that have dominated interest in perennials since the 1960s. They are remarkably robust, adaptable and free-flowering, and compete well with weeds, making them ideal for the wilder style of border. Their disadvantage is that many look untidy after flowering, which may not be a problem in the wilder stretches of the garden, but in the high-visibility border is not ideal. Combining them with upright, later-flowering plants makes obvious sense.

As summer turns to autumn, and then autumn to winter, the flowers gradually fade, and seed heads take over. Seed heads, and their precious cargo of genetic material, are what flowering is all about. Traditionally disregarded as a source of interest, they actually have enormous potential as a source of late-season and winter beauty, at least until winter storms and driving rain batter them down, or they get crushed by snow. Even wind and snow, however, leave some perennials unscathed, such as the taller eupatoriums. On the whole, though, grasses are physically stronger than forbs.

Seed heads are seen at their best in low sunlight, which is rich in wavelengths at the warm end of the spectrum. This means that borders need to be positioned so that they will be struck by sunlight preferably in the late afternoon. Such positioning is also vital to get the best from some woody plants, such as those varieties of dogwood (*Cornus*) and willow (*Salix*) with young bark that glows red, orange or yellow. These are ideal companions for grasses and perennial seed heads if there is enough space.

Opposite Shrubby plants with grey or silver foliage are a good accompaniment to the russet tones of autumn. Species of phlomis, such as this P. *italica* in the Oxfordshire garden of Isabella van Groeningen and Gabriella Pape, have solid seed heads, adding to their value in the autumn and winter garden.

Right Seed heads can be an endless source of fascination, especially when viewed close up: an echinacea species (*top left*); *Succisella inflexa* (*top right*); and *Veronicastrum virginicum* (*bottom left*). The fluffy seeds of many members of the daisy family, such as this aster (*bottom right*) are designed to be blown away on the wind, but for a few weeks they provide splashes of light in the late border.

Digitalis ferruginea

Rosa 'Scharlachglut'

Chamerion angustifolium 'Album'

Anthriscus sylvestris 'Ravenswing'

Plants for Prairies and Borders

Top left Of all the foxgloves, *Digitalis ferruginea* is the most elegant, with tall (up to 1.8 m or 6 ft), narrow spikes of intricately marked brown, yellow and cream flowers, followed by similarly proportioned seed heads. In the right conditions (light or stony soils) the species can self-seed to produce great colonies of these perfectly vertical spires.

Top right *Rosa* 'Scharlachglut' (R. 'Scarlet Fire') with *Stipa gigantea* in the background. Mixing grasses with hybrid roses is unconventional, but since roses tend to look very unattractive after flowering and the tones of the grass complement many rose colours so well, this combination should perhaps be tried more often.

Bottom left *Chamerion angustifolium* 'Album' has spikes of pure white. It is a form of a notoriously running weed (often known as willowherb or fireweed), but it illustrates a very important point about such plants: that this habit is only a problem in the conventional border. When surrounded by other strong-growing plants it behaves much better.

Bottom right *Anthriscus sylvestris* 'Ravenswing' veils an allium hybrid. 'Ravenswing' is a dark form of a plant that, until this sudden mutation was noticed and became fashionable in the 1990s, was almost universally despised as a weed. Cow parsley, as it is commonly known, is one of the most widely distributed wild flowers in Britain, and is clearly able to compete with grasses on roadside verges. However, it is not particularly competitive in the garden, and can be allowed to spread itself around without too much fear of it swamping other plants; one reason for this is that it becomes dormant in July. All four images on the page opposite show Dan Pearson's garden at Home Farm in Northamptonshire.

Top left *Rosa glauca* and *Leucanthemum vulgare*. The rose (still often called by its previous name of *R. rubrifolia*) is a vigorous species that forms a large sprawling shrub with, unusually for a rose, attractive grey foliage – which is the main reason for growing it. It is ideal in large borders or wild gardens, as in this planting by Dan Pearson.

Top right A classic old-fashioned type of shrub rose, 'Stanwell Perpetual', with *Anthriscus sylvestris* 'Ravenswing', in a planting by Dan Pearson.

Middle left The Shirley strain of field poppy (*Papaver rhoeas*) was bred in Surrey, England, by a late Victorian priest and pioneer geneticist, the Reverend Wilks. A variety of pinks and whites was the result. An annual, the field poppy and its varieties can be very successful if mixed with perennials. They are particularly useful in the first year of a new planting, when there are many gaps between the permanent

residents of the border, as they create a splash of colour but not so much leaf and stem growth that slow-growing perennials are swamped. These are at the Clock House in Oxfordshire.

Middle right The thistle-like perennial *Eryngium alpinum* thrives on moist but well-drained soils. It is joined here, in Nori and Sandra Pope's garden at Hadspen in Somerset, by *Nigella damascena*, an annual that, like many from the Mediterranean, does best if sown in the autumn to grow slowly over the winter. It also frequently self-sows.

Bottom *Echinacea purpurea* is loved by insects as well as gardeners. It flowers in late summer and early autumn. Very much a pioneer plant, it tends to dominate newly sown prairies until being displaced by longer-lived plants.

Rosa glauca

Rosa 'Stanwell Perpetual'

Papaver rhoeas

Eryngium alpinum

Echinacea purpurea

Echinacea purpurea

Sanguisorba officinalis

Left By nature a plant of wet grasslands, *Sanguisorba officinalis* thrives in most garden soils, so long as it does not get too dry. Its dark-red, bobble-shaped flower heads are unusual and, because they are spaced far apart on the stems, subtle in impact. These are in a planting by Cleve West in Normandy.

Bottom left *Iris sibirica* with an allium hybrid in a planting by Jinny Blom. Naturally a plant of wet meadows and swamps, *I. sibirica* is amazingly adaptable, thriving on most soils in full sun. It is a good wild-garden plant as its dead leaves form a dense carpet around the young shoots, suppressing competition.

Bottom, middle *Veronicastrum virginicum* is a perennial that flowers in the early summer but has a strong structure that is useful for a long time afterwards. It tends to grow slowly but its tight clump is very long-lived. These were planted by Piet Oudolf at RHS Wisley in Surrey.

Bottom right *Eryngium yuccifolium* is a plant of moist prairie habitats. As with many other eryngiums, the spiky, thistle-like form creates interest among softer-looking plants. It is particularly striking when grown with grasses, as here, by Piet Oudolf at RHS Wisley in Surrey.

Opposite, top These small beds in a planting by Jinny Blom in Gloucestershire are an unusual and attractive variant on the border theme. They have the advantage that the plants can be seen from many different angles. They particularly suit plants with light, intermingling growth. In the left foreground is *Cirsium rivulare* 'Atropurpureum'. The purple on the left of the centre bed is *Salvia verticillata* 'Purple Rain', the scattered cerise *Lychnis flos-jovis*, the apricot spires an eremurus hybrid and the blue on the right *Geranium* 'Kashmir Blue'.

Opposite, bottom left The goldenrods have a mixed reputation, owing to the invasive tendencies of a few species, notably *Solidago grandiflora* and *S. canadensis*. However, they are invaluable for late-season colour, and there are a great many very good garden plants among them. *S. rugosa* is one of the best.

Opposite, bottom, middle left *Baptisia australis* is one of several legumes that play a key role in prairies. It is slow to get going as it invests very heavily in an enormous root system, which, once in place, enables the plant to survive difficult conditions.

Opposite, bottom, middle *Aconitum napellus* is one of the monkshoods, a group of long-lived perennials, most of which originate in mountainous areas of Europe and Asia. They need moist but well-drained and fertile soils. Most form solid clumps once established.

Iris sibirica

Veronicastrum virginicum

Eryngium yuccifolium

Below, middle right A white form of *Aster ericoides*, a North American species of dry prairie habitats. In the garden it and its various colour forms (pinks and blues) are among the very last plants to be flowering in the autumn.

Below, right *Silphium laciniatum* is another very slow-growing but resilient and long-lived prairie plant. Its large, leathery leaves are quite unlike those of any other prairie or border perennial, and are especially appreciated in the autumn.

Cirsium rivulare 'Atropurpureum', *Salvia verticillata* 'Purple Rain', *Lychnis flos-jovis*, *Eremurus* and *Geranium* 'Kashmir Blue'

Solidago rugosa

Baptisia australis

Aconitum napellus

Aster ericoides

Silphium laciniatum

Trees and Woodland

W OODLAND WAS ONCE THE PREDOMINANT vegetation on much of the earth's landmass. In clearing so much for agriculture and settlement, the human race has created conditions much more to our liking, for we have an ambiguous relationship with trees and woodland. There is something primeval about mature woodland; it is a habitat in which we wonder at the majesty and diversity of nature, but at the same time do not feel quite at home. It is almost as if there is an aspect of the collective unconscious that makes us feel on edge when surrounded by trees. This is reflected on a domestic scale by the mixed feelings with which we regard existing trees in our gardens or our neighbours' gardens. We admire fine specimens, welcome their shade in the summer, and see their loss as a local eco-catastrophe; but their shade and questing roots may make gardening beneath them difficult, they may overshadow windows, and there is always the danger that they might fall.

Woodlands are complex habitats, and it takes time to learn to read them. The trees grow in different layers, as does the vegetation towards ground level. There may be a great deal of clarity, with ranks of identical trunks, or there may be a confused mass of understorey shrubs, climbers, ground-cover plants and fallen trees. There may also be a great deal of variation in the amount of vegetation on the ground. We need to consider how gardeners can realize the potential of trees and woodland, a task that sometimes involves making the most of difficult conditions.

The first point to consider is: do you have trees or a woodland? This is another way of asking which came

Previous page Gnarled pomegranate trees remind us of the antiquity of farming on the land that is now occupied by an Italian garden by Dan Pearson. However, the knowledge of old methods of pruning will still be required in years to come in order to maintain the trees in good shape. A variety of wild-flower species grow in their shade; other spring-flowering perennial species can easily be added.

Opposite and left It is hardly woodland, yet this garden by James van Sweden shares with many other town gardens at least one of the features of woodland habitats: shade, cast by trees and large shrubs, but also by walls and buildings. Shrubs are useful for creating privacy and making 'green walls', so important in crowded and stressful urban environments. Planting will have to reflect the amount of sun that reaches the ground: the *Pennisetum* grass (*opposite*) needs sun, but elsewhere shade and root competition make the selection of such appropriate woodland plants as ferns and sedges essential. Notice also how in shade grass is replaced by small, leafy, creeping plants (*left*).

Above An aerial view of a small London garden by Ross Palmer emphasizes how the continuity provided by foliage is important in small spaces. In environments where there may often not be enough light for healthy grass growth, or where there is too much foot-traffic, decking makes a good alternative to a lawn and an effective foil for lush shades of green.

first, the garden or the trees. Trees planted in gardens usually have some ornamental qualities, or have been planted with gardening in mind. If they have not, and are simply too large, cast too much shade or otherwise create problems, then consider thinning – either removing some altogether, or having a tree surgeon take off lower branches to let in more light. Gardens that have been carved out of existing forest will have a more natural selection of trees, which in all probability will be part of a local ecosystem. Managing this ecosystem is part of the responsibility of the gardener: young trees of the same species (as well as ornamentals) should be planted, or natural seedlings encouraged, in order to help the forest regenerate.

There are often advantages to gardening on the edge of natural forest: it is highly likely that the soft, moisture-retaining layer of humus that is the natural upper layer of many wooded environments will still be in place, making growing woodland plants much easier; and it is likely that there will be forest-floor wild flowers and shrubs already growing healthily – the basis of your natural garden!

Left Bluebells (*Hyacinthoides non-scripta*) begin to flower in the light shade beneath coppiced hazel (*Corylus avellana*) in Monty and Sarah Don's own garden in Gloucestershire. Coppicing involves cutting the trees down to near ground level every few years (between ten and thirty-five), with the result that light conditions below them are constantly changing, encouraging the development of a rich flora. Domestically, the cycle can be shortened to a partial cut-back every few years, giving a harvest of straight poles with many uses around the garden.

Opposite At Derrynane House in County Kerry, Ireland, the woodland is in early middle age (notice how none of the tree trunks is particularly wide) and open enough to let in plenty of light to allow plants to grow on the ground; however, this growth is quite low and sparse, indicating an infertile soil. Gardening in woodland conditions can be very rewarding, as some of the most beautiful forest-floor plants (such as trilliums, arisaemas and asarums) grow best in the humus-rich soils of established woodland. A more fertile soil would result in the growth of taller, more vigorous plants, which would smother them.

Creating gardens in places where there are already wild plants demands sensitivity. Gardening operations must ensure that existing species will not be damaged, while plant introductions must not overwhelm the wildlings. A good rule is simply to introduce plants that are clearly related or very similar to those already there. Ground-level species of mature woodland are often evergreen, with wide, glossy leaves. Others are bulbous or emerge early in the year before the trees have grown leaves, retreating underground soon after the summer leaf canopy cuts down light and rain and the soil begins to dry out. Such mature woodland species tend to be slow-growing (and consequently expensive from nurseries). Trilliums are a good example: they do not recover from damage well, and can be severely stressed by tree-cutting operations, disturbance or changes in conditions. They need to be treated with respect.

Plants of the woodland edge or of younger woodland tend to be more vigorous, often strikingly so. They need more nutrients and more light. Geraniums and hellebores, for example, recover more quickly from disturbance and can often spread vigorously, either by shoots at the base or by seeding.

Trees vary greatly in the effect they have on plants growing beneath them. Evergreen conifers, by cutting

Left A woodland of young beech (*Fagus sylvatica*) in a Wisconsin garden by Tom Vanderpoel. Beech tends to suppress ground-level growth, partly by casting a dense shade and partly through its slow-to-decay leaf litter. If this is removed and composted, gardening is made easier, especially in areas of better light, such as that seen in the foreground of the top image, where more wild growth can be seen. North American woodland is often species-rich and may already have interesting plants growing naturally on the forest floor, many of them spring-flowering and summer-dormant. The proximity of trees and a natural forest environment was clearly central to the design brief for this house. The first task of the gardener is to do nothing, but wait and observe, to see what grows naturally over the course of a year. Only then should interventions be made.

Left Here, in the same Wisconsin garden (*see opposite*) a substantial shrub understorey has been planted beneath trees. This can be done only when there is enough light and soil moisture to support healthy shrub growth. Note that the trees do not branch until high up: they are 'high canopy', which reduces the amount of shading. Pruning trees in this way makes gardening below them very much easier.

Above An entirely city-bound and artificial habitat, such as Bonnington Square in London, is in some ways analogous to natural woodland, as city trees cast shade and extract moisture from the soil. However, there is rarely any of the moisture-retaining humus that provides such a good material for woodland plants to grow in, and so plants in such environments are particularly prone to drying out.

out light all year round and carpeting the ground in needles (which are slow to decay), create the most difficult conditions. Deciduous oaks (species of *Quercus*) tend to create the best conditions, for their leaf litter decays quickly to build up a humus layer that is very attractive for many plants to grow in. The other factors that affect the feasibility of gardening beneath trees are the availability of water and of nutrients. Vigorously growing trees may rob the soil of both, but a high water table or high rainfall may compensate for losses of moisture, and a fertile soil for nutrient losses. There is, in fact, a simple rule that helps with understanding what will grow beneath trees. Plants need three things: light, water and nutrients. They can survive with a reduction in one if the other two are at a moderate or high level.

Therefore, it is surprising what will grow in shade on moist and fertile soils, but dry shade is a problem for gardeners because two out of the three requirements are in short supply.

The best garden shade habitat is that which is moist, particularly if nutrient levels are not so high that tall and rampant wild plants are encouraged to spread. Moist shade gives the opportunity to grow the queens of woodland gardens: ferns. Many other very attractive plants, such as species of astilbe, hosta, actaea and primula, will also flourish. The worst is dry shade, where only a limited range of species will thrive, often such tough-looking evergreens as the slow-growing shrubby ruscus or leathery-leaved bergenia.

Conditions often change dramatically during the year, usually becoming more difficult for low-growing plants from the spring onwards. The reason for this is that early in the year, light comes through bare branches and trees do not extract much moisture from the soil. During the summer, light levels below the trees drop and the soil's moisture content becomes progressively lower. This is why most woodland plants are spring-flowering. There is compensation, however: foliage quality.

Opposite, left A clump of mixed woodland is one of the most attractive ways of growing trees, especially in the autumn, when the differences between species are most visible. At Hatfield House in Hertfordshire, evergreen pines grow with larches (*Larix decidua*, a deciduous conifer) and beeches (*Fagus*). Such combinations have often been planted as windbreaks, as they are inherently more resilient than clumps of one species, where 'all the eggs are in one basket'.

Opposite, right Orchards are attractive in their own right, with blossom in the spring and fruit in the autumn. The trees are usually spaced widely enough to allow plenty of light to reach the ground. However, there is a conflict of interest between growing fruit and having wild flowers beneath, as the former needs high fertility, and the latter low. Gardening often presents this sort of dilemma! This orchard is in a garden by Cleve West, in Normandy.

Left Trees in areas with hot summers – such as California, where this garden by Isabelle Greene is located – play a very important role in shading gardens and their users. It is particularly important in such situations to avoid damage to the root system during construction work.

Because of their need to extract maximum light in difficult conditions, many shade plants have wide leaves, which we tend to find attractive. Many are evergreen, too, to maximize light collection during the winter – another boon for the gardener. Temperate monsoon climates, such as Japan and New Zealand and, to a lesser extent, eastern North America, present fewer summer drought problems to woodland plants, and as a consequence have rich woodland floras. Elsewhere, these plants need moist shade if they are to be successful.

Shade and thirsty tree roots can create problems. But it is important to remember a key fact about gardening: natural-style gardening is actually much easier in many ways in shade than it is in full sun. Habitats in full sun are dominated by plants that can use the plentiful light to grow vigorously – especially grasses. Grasses dominate open temperate zone habitats unless the soil is very poor. Cast just a little shade, and grass growth begins to suffer, as you can observe in just about any public park by looking at the sparse grass that grows below trees. A little more shade and grass essentially gives up, and shade-tolerant species can then spread without competition. Woodland plants vary greatly in how quickly they spread, but a great many can be encouraged to do so without too much concern about them competing with each other. Those with very

Left A selection of woodland-edge flora carpets the ground in my own garden. The dark flowers are one of the many fascinating colour variations shown by *Helleborus* × *hybridus*. They are picked up by the dark young foliage of *Lysimachia ciliata* 'Firecracker', which in the conventional border tends to be an aggressive clump-former. Here, however, growing closely with many other plants, it can only infiltrate gaps. A range of smaller daffodil varieties (rather than large-flowered ones) helps keep up the natural look.

Opposite, left A path wends its way through a lightly shaded area of woodland at Derrynane House in Ireland. Elegantly unfurling fern fronds are a large part of the interest here, along with bluebells (*Hyacinthoides non-scripta*).

Opposite, right Bluebells can successfully cover large areas of ground over time; unlike many other bulbs, they flower from seed relatively quickly. They often do best on sandy or acidic soils, and their continued spread and long-term survival is dependent on a number of factors. One is light levels: if too much shade develops, their growth will be suppressed, but with too much light, grass may thrive, displacing the bluebells. The other factor is the growth of taller ground-cover – usually brambles – which shades out bluebell foliage. An annual cut-back of such growth, using a brushcutter, is the most effective way of maintaining bluebells. There are several species, all of them plants of the western fringes of Europe. However, many other bulbs or spring-flowering, summer-dormant plants fill a similar ecological niche in woodland or woodland-edge habitats elsewhere, and tend to require the same management.

wide-spreading stems or roots, such as the periwinkles (species of *Vinca*), are capable of smothering a lot else in their path, and so are useful for filling difficult spaces, but few are this vigorous.

The fact that most shade-lovers spread, but only slowly, means that it is possible to combine them to form attractive tapestries of foliage, generally at a height of between 20 and 60 cm (8–24 in). Such combinations are much more difficult to achieve in open sunny conditions. Over a large scale, the low level of this planting may seem monotonous, and that is where the occasional fern comes in useful: ferns have a height and a distinctive habit ideal for punctuating low-level foliage. Not all require moist shade: a few flourish robustly in drier conditions, including *Dryopteris filix-mas*

Left and below, left Daffodils (species and hybrids of *Narcissus*) are very successful when naturalized – planted in sun or light shade and allowed to spread by themselves. Those pictured opposite are a wild species, *Narcissus pseudonarcissus*, while those below are a selection of strong-growing hybrids planted by John Brookes in Sussex. While both create a beautiful and very low-maintenance spectacle, it is really only the wild species, or small varieties raised from them, that look 'natural'.

Below, right A wood in the outer reaches of the garden by Dan Pearson at Home Farm in Northamptonshire, where the wild cow parsley (*Anthriscus sylvestris*) grows in profusion. Maintenance here consists of regularly mowing a path through and cutting back the wild flowers with a brushcutter once a year. Mowing paths through existing vegetation is one of the most attractive ways to turn what might otherwise be seen as dull or rank growth into something more intentional, and therefore more likely to be seen as worth appreciating.

and several species of polystichium (*Polystichium setiferum*, *P. munitum* and *P. acrostichoides*).

Bulbs can be mixed into woodland ground flora, to flower in the spring and die back in the summer. Sedges (species of *Carex*) are particularly useful, too; much like grasses, but slower growing, they work well in shade plantings. There are a great many species and varieties in cultivation now, but any with green foliage less than 30 cm (1 ft) tall are almost certainly going to be good woodland plants. The main rule with mixing shade plants is to get a feel for the distinction between slower-growing, more shade-tolerant woodlanders and the more expansive, stronger-growing, woodland-edge ones. The former are nearly always evergreen, or have leathery, long-lived leaves, or (like bulbs) die back in early summer.

Gardens change over time. Those with young trees will change particularly quickly, and dramatically. As the trees grow, they will shade the ground beneath them, so changing the garden habitat. Species that can spread, either by forming extensive clumps or by self-sowing, will adapt; others, particularly true woodland species, will be less able to. Here, gardeners can learn something from traditional woodland management practices: in many parts of Europe, large areas of woodland have traditionally been managed as coppice, where trees have been cut down to regrow from the stumps, on a rotational basis. The result has been the development of a flora of more adaptable woodland species, able either to grow in varied light conditions or to spread quickly when tree-felling brings more light to the woodland floor. One lesson is that adaptable species are needed beneath young trees; another is that there are possibilities for developing ornamental coppice. Many trees can be kept small through regular cutting back to the base, and if they are combined with plants of lightly shaded habitats, such as foxgloves and geraniums, the result can be a diverse and varied low-maintenance combination.

Paths that dip into and out of shade create a sense of mystery, always attractive in a garden. At Dan Pearson's garden at Home Farm in Northamptonshire, a climbing honeysuckle (a species of *Lonicera*) is well-established on a tree (*above*). Such climbers are an essential part of natural forest and woodland-edge habitats; in the garden they are a good example of how space may be used 'twice over'. Many provide good habitat for birds. The yellow–green flower is *Alchemilla mollis*, a meadow plant of central Europe, where its stems grow stretched out among the grasses. It also thrives in light shade, where in the absence of grass its growth is completely different, and it forms dense clumps. More open areas among trees, where sunlight penetrates for at least part of the day, provide habitat for taller, more vigorous plants than are typical of full shade (*right*). The dense carpet of broad, ground-hugging leaves in the foreground illustrates a habit that is characteristic of shade-tolerant plants.

Below The white flowers are on a grass-like plant, the wood rush *Luzula sylvatica*, which is extremely useful as ground cover below trees. The gaps between the paving stones are filled by a strawberry lookalike, *Duchesnea indica*. Using a ground-cover plant in paving helps to reduce the germination of weed seeds.

Right Geraniums (this is *G. psilostemon*) are vigorous and rewarding plants that are highly adaptable. Nearly all are happy in full sun – so long as they are not liable to suffer prolonged drought – and also in at least light shade. Both the gardens pictured on this page are by Dan Pearson.

Left A range of grasses and sun-loving wild flowers among young trees. As the trees grow the habitat will change, and such plants are liable to die out, to be replaced by those more adapted to shade. Tom Vanderpoel designed this Wisconsin garden.

Below The elegant, narrow spikes of *Digitalis ferruginea* in front of a purple-leaved hazel, *Corylus maxima* 'Purpurea', in a planting by Jinny Blom. The pink flowers in front are *Veronicastrum virginicum*. The foxglove is short-lived but readily self-sows, and like that of many species of woodland-edge habitats its lifestyle has evolved to deal with changing light conditions. Hazels are happy in light shade, beneath larger deciduous trees. Traditionally they have often been managed for coppice to produce multi-stemmed

specimens, and they respond well to being regularly cut down to the base.

Right, top At Broughton Hall in Yorkshire, Dan Pearson has used a periwinkle (*Vinca minor*) as ground cover below young trees. It will be happy with the relatively dark shade beneath the trees as they establish. Although they can cope with fairly low light levels, the ferns (*Dryopteris filix-mas*) may eventually lose out as the shade increases.

Right, bottom Climbers are an important part of woodland-edge habitats. In gardens, they can be encouraged to scramble up trees, as with this climbing rose in Isabelle van Groeningen and Gabriella Pape's Oxfordshire garden. At ground level is a pink-flowered variety of *Lamium maculatum*, the dead-nettle.

Plants in town gardens often experience many of the same environmental factors that occur in woodland: shade and drought. The drought is generally because of the 'rain shadow' effect caused by buildings. It may, however, also be because of poor-quality soil; soils in urban areas have often been modified or damaged, or are full of foundations and rubble. Only rarely do established trees in town gardens have beneath them the thick layer of humus-rich soil that is characteristic of woodland, and which supports true woodland plants. Where soils have been particularly badly damaged, or are of very low quality, raised beds of imported soil may be the only way to create a good rooting environment.

The planting of shaded urban gardens needs to reflect these additional problems of possible drought and soil poverty. Particularly valuable are those plants that combine a robust nature with evergreen foliage, or at least attractive foliage for the entire growing season. Urban gardens are almost inevitably small, and in such

Opposite Bamboos are one of the most attractive and useful plants for small spaces in the city, as here, in Jinny Blom's own garden. However, many have vigorous, questing root systems, which can upset neighbourly relations. Use non-running species, or restrain plants behind barriers made of paving slabs buried vertically.

Left Shade cast by city buildings has here prompted Dan Pearson to create a woodland feel by using plants typical of wooded habitats. The white flowers of *Amelanchier canadensis* will be followed by dark-purple berries (rapidly eaten by birds) and striking yellow–orange autumn colour. At ground level are a variety of ground-covering woodland-edge species, including *Luzula sylvatica*.

Right, top Box (*Buxus sempervirens*) is one of the few shrubs that can thrive in shade; being evergreen it can make the most of winter's leafless branches. These box have been planted beneath trained apple trees. However, their proximity will reduce the apples' fruiting potential, as box is notoriously greedy. In keeping with the soft outlines of this lightly managed country garden by Jinny Blom, they are loosely shaped rather than hard pruned.

Right, bottom Vines (*Vitis vinifera*) trained along horizontal wires give shade in Mediterranean climates. The fig (*Ficus carica*) is commonly trained as a wall shrub. Using shrubs in this way gives a greener, more rustic feel to urban gardens dominated by hard vertical surfaces. This is David and Judy Drew's own garden in France.

a space it is all the more important that plants earn
their keep, so foliage quality and longevity are much
appreciated. Where there is sufficient soil moisture,
ferns and hostas have much to offer. In drier conditions,
plants that tolerate some drought – such as many sedges
(*Carex*) or heuchera, with their variety of patterned and
coloured leaves – will be very useful. Even in a small
garden, repetition is important in order to achieve the
natural look. Sedges are very useful for this: clumps of
their linear leaves repeated across a garden create links
through space, and because they are evergreen, make
links through time, too.

Given that many urban gardens are dominated by
walls, shrubs and climbers have an important role to
play. A wall covered with the greenery of climbing plants
rapidly becomes something other than a wall in the
mind's eye. Vegetated walls are much appreciated by
urban wildlife too. Shrubs help to break up space,
creating multiple viewpoints and hidden areas. Many
tend to have an expansive and amorphous habit, so
pruning may be necessary in order to keep them
to a size and shape that works in the available space.
Pruning away lower branches can create more space
for underplanting with perennials and bulbs, and also
brings the advantage of allowing a better view of the
lower stems, which can be attractive in their own right.
Shrubs trained against walls tend to create a thicker and
lusher effect than that produced by climbers.

Right and opposite, left and top right
Mature trees are irreplaceable, so
every effort should be made to
preserve them when changes are
made. Sometimes it is possible to
design garden or other features
around them. These gardens are
by Graham Pockett (*right*), Luis
Vallejo (*opposite, left*) and Cleve
West (*opposite, top right*).

Opposite, bottom right Old (and
strong) trees can become
garden features in so many
ways. Very large specimens can
support tree houses, and those
with large horizontal branches
swings (as in this garden by
Jinny Blom) and Tarzan ropes.

Some gardens will include a tree or trees of great value both to the garden environment and to the surroundings, and worth any amount of effort and expenditure to preserve and cherish. In others, decisions may have to be made, and trees removed or planted.

A tree will almost certainly outlive the person who plants it. Planting a tree can also have an effect on the neighbourhood far greater than anything else we do in the garden. Given the impact that a tree has on the space around it, the selection of species appropriate for a natural-style garden is very important. There is a strong case for planting locally native trees in many places, because they can be relied on to survive the vagaries of the local climate. They will also create a sense of belonging, forge a link with the surroundings – as I shall explore in 'Gardens and the Wider Landscape',

Above The white bark of birch (species of *Betula*) is one of the most powerful tree images for those at cooler latitudes, especially in the winter. These birches are grown by Kenneth and June Ashburner at Stone Lane Gardens in Devon.

Right The management of this planting of poplars in a Belgian garden by Paul Deroose – almost a stylized woodland – ensures that nothing taller than grass will grow. Unnatural-looking it may be, but it has an austere beauty that makes the most of the trees' distinctively patterned bark.

below – and are usually more valuable to wildlife than non-native ones.

Many of the trees marketed by the nursery industry for the domestic garden are small-growing, and selected or bred to be highly ornamental. Many ornamental tree varieties look distinctly unnatural, with variegated foliage, constricted shapes or, especially, bright or double flowers. Pale or subtly coloured flowers are far more the norm in nature (at least in temperate regions) than very bright ones, and yet the overall effect of such flowers is no less beautiful. Double flowers are often double at the expense of nectar-producing organs, so hold little interest for bees and other insects.

If careful thought is given to the eventual size of a tree and its impact on the garden and – perhaps more crucially – neighbouring gardens, the planting of long-lived and large trees can be of very real long-term benefit. Such trees do not need to be broad-canopied if room does not allow; some forms of commercially available native species occupy less space than those from the normal gene pool. An excellent example is the narrow form of the English oak, Quercus robur f. fastigiata, which has all the considerable wildlife benefits of the species but takes up less space and casts less shade.

Conventional tree-planting practice generally puts a single tree into a space to stand in splendid isolation. A walk in woodland soon shows that few trees grow in this way; they grow at varying distances from each other, and many are not straight, or have odd shapes. Nature is not regular. A more natural effect in gardens can be created by planting several trees close together, or even several in one planting hole, resulting in an interesting multi-stem effect. 'Mini-woodlands', with multiples of several different species planted close together, can be surprisingly successful, so long as no very fast-growing species are included.

Trees and Plants for Woodland Gardens

Birches (species of *Betula*) are supremely useful trees for gardens, being small to medium-sized, casting a light shade and having the most wonderfully decorative bark, which is particularly appreciated in the winter. However, they do have one major disadvantage: their shallow roots drain the soil around them of moisture and nutrients. They are particularly valuable for cold or exposed places, or shallow or rocky soils.

Betula utilis var. *jacquemontii* (*below left*) has one of the whitest barks. *B. nigra* (*bottom left*), known in North America as river birch for its habit of growing along rivers or in wet ground, is unusual among birches for its distinctively shaggy bark. Not all species have white bark, though, as can be seen from *B. ermanii* 'Grayswood Hill' and *B. delavayi* (*below, middle and right*). Birch flowers (*bottom right*) are very attractive in themselves, especially as they are often among the first to appear at the end of the winter.

Betula utilis var. jacquemontii

B. ermanii 'Grayswood Hill'

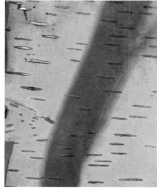
B. delavayi

B. nigra

Betula sp.

Amelanchier canadensis

Tellima grandiflora

Left, top Amelanchier canadensis is a first-class garden tree or large shrub, particularly for cold or wet ground. White flowers in the spring are followed by dark-purple berries in the summer – much appreciated by birds. The orange autumn leaf colour is spectacular and reliable.

Left, bottom A useful plant for relatively dry shade, Tellima grandiflora is perhaps best described as 'subtle', and most effective grown in large groups – something it often achieves through its habit of frequent self-sowing.

Right, top Pears should be appreciated for their early spring flowers as much as their fruit. This one is Pyrus communis 'Belle de Soignies'.

Right, middle Arum italicum 'Marmoratum' is a useful source of colour. As with many woodland plants of Mediterranean origin, it starts to make growth very early, to accompany snowdrops and other early bulbs. Late summer sees it produce colourful spikes of glossy orange berries.

Right, bottom Snowdrops (this is the common Galanthus nivalis) are some of the most valued of woodland bulbs for their early flower and rapid rate of increase. They are suitable for spaces under deciduous trees where little else will grow, and for combining with perennials in borders, flowering long before most perennials emerge.

Pyrus communis 'Belle de Soignies'

Arum italicum 'Marmoratum'

Galanthus nivalis

Dicentra spectabilis 'Alba'

Malus 'Cox's Orange Pippin'

Corydalis flexuosa

Cercis canadensis 'Forest Pansy'

Top left Dicentra spectabilis 'Alba' makes a display of lustrous white flowers in late spring. It needs a moist but well-drained and fertile soil in light shade. Gardeners also need to remember that it tends to die back at midsummer. The spotted leaves are those of another woodlander that is usually summer-dormant, a form of *Pulmonaria officinalis*.

Top right 'Cox's Orange Pippin' is renowned as one of the most richly flavoured of all apples. Like many apples, however, it only performs well in ideal conditions. The lesson is that where tree fruit is concerned, it pays to buy from a local nursery that sells only varieties likely to do well in the area.

Bottom left Corydalis flexuosa is one of several corydalis species with exquisitely true-blue flowers and delicate, maidenhair-fern-like foliage. It flowers in the spring to early summer, and needs moist but well-drained soil.

Bottom right Cercis canadensis 'Forest Pansy' is a small tree with leaves that are a rich purple–bronze. Some leaves reflect light, while others glow with backlighting. Being an 'understorey' tree – one that grows beneath the larger dominant trees of the forest – it needs shelter from wind.

Euonymus europaeus

Rubus fruticosus

Above, left Species of euonymus are useful small trees for gardens, especially on alkaline soil. They are also frequently found as a minor component in traditional mixed hedges. They often go unnoticed until the autumn, when they suddenly seize the attention with masses of bright-pink fruits, inside which glow orange seeds.

Above, right The blackberry is a plant about which we tend to feel ambivalent, cursing its spiny stems thrust over more decorative plants for most of the year, but loving to collect its tasty and succulent fruits in the autumn. It can be grown in wilder parts of the garden, to scramble harmlessly over large shrubs or traditional mixed hedges.

Right The pale-pink flowers of *Astrantia major* var. *rosea* are produced in flushes from early summer to early autumn. The wild form has off-white flowers, while some forms, such as 'Claret', are a wonderfully rich dark red. It thrives in moist soils in light shade, and prefers a cool climate.

Far right Cornus alba 'Kesselringii' is one of many dogwoods that make good garden plants. All *C. alba* varieties grow best in damp soils, and should be cut back frequently in order to produce plenty of the brightly coloured bark that is one of their great joys.

Astrantia major var. *rosea*

Cornus alba 'Kesselringii'

S CULPTURE HAS BEEN AN IMPORTANT ELEMENT in gardens for centuries, and as garden culture grows to be ever more sophisticated, and consumers wealthier, more people are buying sculpture or other artworks for the garden. Or they are creating their own, stimulated and empowered by courses, workshops and books on a steadily increasing range of techniques. Garden art should not just be thought of in terms of purely decorative objects, however. Many functional elements of the garden can be beautiful, too; indeed, a characteristic that really sets a garden apart from the ordinary and pedestrian is the presence of garden buildings and other functional structures that are individually designed or made, or imaginatively decorated, rather than standard 'off the peg' products.

Natural-style gardeners will probably want any sculpture and ornamental elements to fit in with their general theme. They will also almost certainly want them to be made from materials that fit into the ethos of the garden, that of sustainability and respect for the earth. Plastics, metal and other materials that depend on high levels of processing and which jar with their natural surroundings will often be rejected by those who want a naturalistic garden. One appealing aspect of the use of natural materials is that it is often possible to use materials produced on site: wood from trees already growing in the garden, or clay subsoil dug from the ground.

Ornaments and structures made from natural materials using pre-industrial processes are qualitatively different from industrial ones: they will eventually biodegrade (if living) or weather, corrode and disintegrate (if non-living). In some ways this can be a disadvantage, but for the earth, and future generations, it is a great advantage: what comes from the earth and goes back to the earth will not cause a disposal problem. In addition, the very process of decay can be an interesting feature of the work itself.

Previous page Natural materials are vital for the natural-style garden. Such enigmatic sculptures as these spheres, in a garden by Cleve West in Normandy, remind us of the sculptural and artistic properties of all natural environments.

Above Stone planters complement a willow fencing panel at Petersham House, Surrey. The fence has been made of vertical rods two to three years old and one-year-old horizontal wands. It illustrates the rich variety of colours of young willow bark.

Right 'Enigmatic' is the key word for much contemporary nature-inspired sculpture. *Thread* by Alasdair Currie is rooted in its surroundings (Wood of Cree, Dumfries & Galloway) yet clearly shaped by human hand.

Above Terracotta is underrated as a sculptural material, yet its earthy tones make it ideal for the natural-style garden. In *Burning Bush* (2000) by Jonathan Garratt, 'flames' are mounted on long steel poles, enabling them to be moved around, so that the owner has the opportunity to rework the piece constantly.

Right The simplest kind of garden seat is seen at a garden by John Brookes in southern England. A tree was left where it fell and given the smallest number of cuts necessary in order to make a seat.

Far right Willow, hazel and other flexible woods can be used to create abstract sculptures, adding an enigmatic dimension wherever they are placed. This is at Woodpeckers in Warwickshire.

In this chapter I look at applications for some of the traditional rural skills that were once commonly practised and used for a wide range of practical purposes, then nearly forgotten and lost, but have now been rediscovered and turned towards uses as much decorative as functional. Of these, two particularly stand out for their garden appeal: the use of willow (species of *Salix*) and other pliable woods for woven structures, and the use of earth for construction. The latter requires great physical strength and skill in judging and using materials, which can take a long time to acquire, but the pliable wooden wands for the former are easy to source and use, and even the wheelchair-bound and children can use them to create successful structures.

In almost all the world's traditional cultures, there are crafts that use the young and very pliable stems of woody plants for a wide range of purposes, from buildings to baskets. In temperate climates, willow reigns supreme, being very easy and quick to grow, and producing (with the right management techniques) plenty of straight rods. The fresh shoots of most willow varieties are amazingly pliable – they can even be tied in knots – and many have very attractive bark colours. After a year outside, the thinnest cut shoots dry out and become brittle; after three years or so, they are so brittle that the slightest disturbance will break them. Thicker shoots will last a little longer, as will the stems of many other species, such as hazel. The longest lasting (well over fifteen years if kept dry) are strips of oak produced by cleaving, or splitting, along the grain of the wood. All these materials are flexible enough, when young, to be woven. Traditionally, thicker pieces would be used to make fences or moveable fence sections (called hurdles) and thinner ones used in basket work.

Below, left, and opposite, top left Willow arches and tunnels are a popular and easy-to-make form of living sculpture. A tunnel could transport the visitor into another part of the garden without their seeing the route – like a cosmological wormhole. These are by Lucy Redman (*below, left*) and at Garden Organic's Yalding site in Kent (*opposite, top left*).

Below, right, and opposite, right Live willow wands are easy to weave into a simple pattern (*opposite, right*). More sophisticated effects are possible using narrower wands and combining them (*below*). Such structures are particularly useful as screens. Both these are in Judy and David Drew's own garden in France.

Willow, however, has another trick up its sleeve. It is remarkably easy to propagate – practically any piece of young stem will root if thrust into the ground in the winter or spring. This, combined with its extreme flexibility, has meant that structures of living willow can be made easily and quickly. Making living willow sculptures became very popular in the 1990s, particularly for community projects, as children can help both build and maintain the sculptures. The size, complexity and sheer inventiveness of some willow sculptures are breathtaking: arches or wigwams or imaginative pergolas, even surreal dragons of curving stems clothed in fresh green leaves bending and winding across the ground, all obviously designed and built but very luxuriantly alive.

What is so marvellous about living willow structures is the shape. Curves and other organic forms are much easier than geometric ones, as a result of the pliability of the material. Once the wands are rooted and actively growing, the shapes into which they have been constructed set and harden, as the stems grow and stiffen.

Below and opposite, top left Animals are a popular subject for sculptures in willow or other pliable wooden materials. Given the expense of sculpture, the use of a preservative to prolong their life does seem advisable. These willow pigs (*below*) are at Merriments Gardens, East Sussex; the sheep (*opposite, top left*) are at Nyewood House in West Sussex.

Above, right Obelisks (these are by Zelie Jopling) are among the easiest willow structures to make. They can be used to support such short-lived climbing plants as sweet peas, such loose scramblers as nasturtiums, or, if made of thicker and more durable wood, perennials, such as clematis. As with all free-standing supports for climbers it is very important that the size of the plants is appropriate for the size of the obelisk. Climbers, even if well-matched, can easily become top-heavy, so it is advisable that an obelisk be firmly attached to the ground, for example by being tied tightly to stakes.

Right The fine open-work interlacing of the wands used for this ornamental backing for a garden seat at RHS Harlow Carr in Yorkshire seems perfect for a garden; it is not so heavy that it imposes itself on its surroundings, but it makes a strong visual impact. An additional practical advantage to light, open structures is that they are less likely to be blown over by the wind.

Left This woven surround for a free-standing turf seat at Helmingham Hall Gardens in Suffolk appears to be an attractive, innovative solution to the problem of how to make a round seat. For the wood not to rot, however, the surround needs to be lined with plastic sheeting before being back-filled with soil.

Opposite, top An innovative use of hurdle-making techniques. The use of very durable timber, such as oak, is imperative, however, as brittle and decaying hurdles in such a position would be a hazard. The bridge is by Robert Yates at Brampton Willows, Suffolk.

Opposite, bottom So long as it is understood that such creations as this are not long-lived (lasting a few years at the most), there is enormous scope for the construction of large-scale, semi-functional garden structures. They are particularly useful for special events. This ornamental gateway is by Stephanie Bunn at the Hannah Peschar Sculpture Garden by Anthony Paul in Surrey.

If kept weed-free at the base, and kept moist during the first summer, willow will take only a year to establish. It grows anywhere that is not drought-prone, and it does not need wet soils.

Living willow sculptures are easily created with enthusiasm, but maintaining them involves rather monotonous work. All new growth *must* be pruned off in the winter, otherwise in no time at all the sculpture will turn into a collection of misshapen trees.

Even with the best maintenance, no professional willow sculptor would expect a piece of work to last

much beyond ten or fifteen years. Whether one invests in sculptures and structures of non-living or living willow, the effects are more temporary than those made of conventional wood, stone or even earth. There is a historical precedent for such short-lifespan structures: the so-called 'carpenter's work' of medieval European gardens, consisting of elaborate structures – arches, arbours and walkways – built out of trellises of wood. They decorated many an aristocratic garden and were replaced every few years. For the modern gardener at home, it has to be said that one of the pleasures of willow and other structures using natural materials is not the end result but the enjoyment and satisfaction of making them.

Structures of non-living wooden wands or similar flexible materials can be made by professionals. However, it is often more fun, more satisfying and cheaper to make them yourself. Obelisks and other vertical supports for climbers are a good type to start off with. They look decorative while the climbers are still small, and are easy to make using a similar technique to basket-making. Hurdling is also relatively easy to learn, and is a particularly useful skill, as hurdle fences are very attractive, especially in country gardens. They do not last long, however. For those who are already reasonably experienced at woodwork, learning such traditional crafts as green-oak carpentry is also a possibility. More difficult skills, such as thatching, are best left to the professionals.

Structures made from non-living willow, or any other wood, are inevitably temporary; that can mean the sudden loss of a hazel-hurdle fence in a storm, or the slow disintegration of an expensive piece of sculpture. Small and moveable works can survive longer if they are

Opposite The arbour is a well-established garden feature, providing shelter from the wind. Its uprights can also be used as supports for light climbing plants.

Right Simple fences like this one by Lesley Rosser can be made with willow wands or similar fine stems attached to sturdy wooden rails with occasional uprights fixed into the ground.

kept under cover during the winter or rainy season, and all such structures will last longer if they are treated with a wood preservative. In the past only relatively toxic and highly persistent chemicals could be used for this purpose, but the wood-preservative market is changing rapidly, and safe products that do not leave long-lived toxic residues in the soil are increasingly available. Those based on natural oils, for example, can delay the process of decay by several years.

Traditionally, materials for hurdling, basket-making and all the other age-old skills that were once vital in rural economies, but which today have been revived for ornamental purposes, depended on particular tree-management techniques. Chief among these were coppicing and pollarding. Coppicing describes the cutting

Left Garden furniture has traditionally been made of durable timber. The less the wood is cut, shaped and reassembled, the more elemental a quality it has, and the more appropriate it is for natural-style spaces. Minimal working, to produce shallow impressions for sitting, preserves the raw quality of the wood used for these seats. The seat in the top image is at Blakenham Woodland Garden in Suffolk; that in the bottom image is in Dan Pearson's garden at Stacey's House, East Sussex.

Opposite, left Sourcing timber in close proximity to where it is to be used is a particularly attractive and eco-friendly aspect of working with natural materials. The straight pieces of wood used here at Blakenham Woodland Garden in Suffolk are the result of such woodland management techniques as coppicing and pollarding.

Opposite, right Wood bleached to look like driftwood has been used by Ben Forgey to create this shelter, which conceals a seat, in James van Sweden's own garden on Chesapeake Bay. Strips of pliable wood tie the pieces together. Its appearance is ideally suited to a coastal garden.

down of trees that are known to regenerate from basal shoots, and the harvesting of these shoots at any time from one to thirty-five years later. In Europe, willow, hazel (species of *Corylus*) and sweet chestnut (*Castanea sativa*) have been the most economically important. New shoots from coppiced trees tend to be very straight, and as such are very useful. Pollarding is a similar process, but the tree (usually a willow) is cut around 2–3 m (6–10 ft) above ground, to produce similar straight and relatively uniform rods at the top of the trunk.

Gardeners in country locations who like to use natural materials should consider planting willows and hazels to produce wood to work with. Willows will produce usable wands within a few years of planting. Coppiced woodland is also a valuable habitat (see pages 76 and 138).

Another old craft that has enjoyed much recent attention is that of earth-building. Traditional cultures all over the world have long built with earth, using a range of techniques, such as ramming earth between shuttering to create walls, shaping mud into bricks (adobe) and mixing subsoil, aggregate and straw to form cob. Rammed earth and cob can both have very attractive colours, depending on the mineral mix in the soil: red–pink or yellow, as well as the expected brown.

There are two very important considerations when constructing with earth: the soil must be of the right consistency (it must have the right proportion of clay and sand particles), and the structure must be protected from damp. Not surprisingly, earth building has become most popular in areas with limited rainfall, such as north Africa and south-west USA. Elsewhere, earth-builders need to remember what is well known in Devon, the UK's cob-building heartland: 'Cob will last a thousand years if it has a good hat, a good coat and a good pair of boots' – a proper roof, rendered walls, and a stone or other waterproof base to lift the earth walls above ground level. For garden structures, the render can be omitted, and instead a roof with relatively wide eaves built to keep off driving rain. Temporary sculptures (which should still last several years) can also be made without a roof.

Of the various earth-building techniques, cob is perhaps the most useful and easiest for the gardener. Cob is a very forgiving material, so a wide range of soil types are suitable. Any subsoil that sets hard when dry can be used, although if there is a high clay content, sand or aggregate must be added. Cob also lends itself to curves – indeed it is difficult to make right-angled corners with it – so it is ideal for natural-looking, flowing shapes.

Cob walls are perfect in natural-style gardens. Their soft colours, flowing shapes and uneven textures look like earth somehow made vertical and sculptural, which is, of course, exactly what they are. They complement flowers

Opposite Such craftsman-made pieces as this driftwood-look chair by Ben Forgey in James van Sweden's own garden are deceptively simple. The amount of work that goes into sourcing timber and then selecting pieces appropriate for a particular project is itself enormous. Their rough-and-ready appearance does not mean they do not need protection and maintenance.

Left, top Scrap timber from sawmills or woodyards can be made into attractively chunky furniture for the natural-style garden, with relatively limited carpentry skills. This bench is in Brockwell Park, south London.

Left, bottom Thatching is a traditional rural skill that is difficult to master, but there is nothing so appropriate for giving a rustic appearance to garden buildings. The building on the right, designed by Charles Morris for Gervase Jackson-Stops at the Menagerie in Northamptonshire, evokes classical architecture but in wood; that on the left, in Blakenham Woodland Garden, Suffolk, by contrast has a self-consciously rustic style, using at least some unshaped, naturally bending elements.

and foliage, and their heat-storage qualities have long been recognized by growers of fruit and vegetables. Large houses in Britain historically had walled kitchen gardens. Building one today is an uneconomic prospect to all but the wealthiest, but cob walls are much cheaper to build, making them an attractive proposition for gardeners. Walls 2–2.5 m (6–8 ft) high can make a substantial impact on microclimate. The material is also ideal for building well-insulated garden sheds and cosy summerhouses, or can be used simply as a sculptural material.

Cob encapsulates the natural approach, being little more than subsoil rearranged for human enjoyment and use. This is the core of the philosophy of ornament in the natural-style garden: that local, biodegradable materials are used, which will leave no visible debris. Visually they complement their area of origin, and those who use them can be sure that they are neither taking anything away nor leaving anything behind. Natural ornament should tread lightly on the earth.

Cob is a first-rate material for garden walls, since it stores heat during the day and radiates it during the night. It is ideal for where fruit is to be grown, or other plants that need protection and heat, or for summerhouses. Here Matt Robinson has used cob walls as features both functional and decorative.

Land and Water Forms

F OR THE GARDENER INSPIRED BY NATURE, the lure of water is irresistible. Visually, water is different from anything else in the garden; ecologically, it offers a useful habitat, or, in fact, several different habitats along the scale from open water to damp soil. Whatever the form water takes in the landscape, one of its attractions is its overall shape and the relationship it has with the rest of the garden. However, that can be the greatest challenge to the gardener: how do you design a body of water for a place where water would not naturally be? A natural-style approach is often the best solution.

Related to the idea of shaping bodies of water is that of shaping the ground: landforms. Both derive from contours to be seen in the natural or cultivated

Previous page An urban water garden by Julie Toll; see page 131.

Below A modernist version of the conventional hard-edged pool, in John Brookes's own garden. The clump of vegetation, however, offers access and cover for wildlife seeking to approach the water. The yellow iris is *Iris pseudacorus*, a species that thrives either in water or in ordinary garden soil; the large leaves are *Petasites japonicus* var. *giganteus*, dramatic and echoing the curve of the water body. But note: it is dangerously invasive! (As is *I. pseudacorus* in North America.) In the eyes of many, organic curving shapes, so frequently

associated with modernism, are far more appropriate for ponds and pools than the straight lines of earlier times.

Right This enigmatic pond, not much larger than the island at its centre, is dominated by a tree that clearly likes to have its roots in water. It is a clever feature. The garden, in Normandy, is by Cleve West.

landscape; both involve shaping the land with similar machinery (now excavators, once armies of men with spades and wheelbarrows); and both make a major impact on their surroundings. The big difference is that the making of ponds is very common, but the conscious sculpting of land is still very rare. Landforming is by no means new: eighteenth-century landscape architects indulged in it on a huge scale, but they usually tried to hide their creations as 'natural' features. Modern landforming grew out of the field of 'land art', and has been given a huge boost by Charles Jencks, with his widely publicized Garden of Cosmic Speculation in Scotland. Most well-known examples are on a large scale, but designers are now developing landforms for smaller gardens.

Opposite Landforms are a very simple way to create amphitheatres, serving a function when a performance space is needed and making a pleasing sculptural moulding of the ground the rest of the time. This one is at Blakenham Woodland Garden in Suffolk.

Right, top Clearly created from the spoil removed when the pond was excavated, this mound has been transformed by Veronique Maria into an enigmatic artwork by the addition of a wicker-lined seating area. To some it might evoke a volcano, to others the mounts of medieval gardens, or the mounds made in Japanese gardens for viewing the moon.

Right, bottom This spiral with a centre of chalk, in Blakenham Woodland Garden in Suffolk, is intended only as an artwork. As with landforms generally, children love playing here.

Simplicity is often the key to success when shaping land and water. Bold organic shapes and uncomplicated sweeping lines create a powerful, immediate impression. Most who seek a natural style will be most determined not to use anything that remotely resembles a straight line. However, there is an important distinction to be made between the shaping of ground with the idea of making it look as though nature arranged it that way, and the land as art-object: the landform as art-object needs to stand out as clearly intentional and therefore artificial. The trick is simply for it not to look *too* artificial.

Left Bold simplicity makes this woodland pond at Dumbarton Oaks in Washington, D.C., stand out. Conventional wisdom is against making ponds under trees, but in fact much pondlife is quite happy out of the sun. Leaves should be skimmed off in the autumn, though.

Above The aim of this perfectly circular pond appears to be simply artistic. It is in fact the remains of a Victorian pool, at Corrour in Scotland (by Jinny Blom). Now it echoes the loch beyond, connecting landscape with garden.

Opposite A bold sweep of decking allows access to seating around a pool in a garden by Dan Pearson. Decking and pools go together well; the wooden surface can be cantilevered out over water, giving a sensation of floating. It also allows views down into deeper water, and, by obscuring the point at which the water meets the bank, handles situations where water levels rise and fall.

Whether the simplicity of the overall form should be extended to planting is another matter. Planting the boundaries or surfaces of either landforms or water arguably obscures them. The impact of a well-designed feature is derived from confrontation, the presence in the landscape of a bold and simple shape. A landform planted with anything other than grass rapidly becomes less obviously a landform – which may be a good thing, if subtlety or surprise is the desired effect. On the whole, however, landforms are most effective if covered simply in mown, or partially mown, grass; indeed, part of the appeal of successful landforms in temperate climates is not just their shape but also their clothing with a garment of trim lawn grass.

A landform is a very simple way of enhancing the character of an open grassed area, and, by obscuring part of it, making it seem bigger than it really is. It can also have functional aspects: providing a slope for children to play on, a shelter from prevailing winds, a suntrap or, most ambitiously, an amphitheatre for events. If landforms are to be regularly used to provide seating, it is possible to design them with terraces, which adds considerably to their visual impact.

Unlike that of making garden ponds, the craft of landforming is not well established. Practical considerations include whether the soil is to be dug from the immediate vicinity or brought in from elsewhere, and the nature of the soil itself. It needs to be free-draining, otherwise waterlogging may become a problem. Conversely, it does need to be reasonably good-quality soil; anything too light or poor may result in the grass becoming dry or sparse in hot summers. On the other hand, poor soil or subsoil can be turned to advantage by clothing the landform in a wild-flower meadow mix rather than regularly mowing.

Landforms and water forms have an obvious point of connection, as digging a pond creates a heap of spoil,

Opposite, top This pool, at Mount Usher Gardens, County Wicklow, Ireland, has been created out of a rocky environment. The surrounding vegetation is lush and exuberant: the large leaves are *Darmera peltata* and the white flowers *Polygonatum multiflorum*. The use of luxuriantly leafy species in damp and shaded places is a way of emphasizing the character of the place and making the most of a situation where plants of such strong character will thrive.

Opposite, bottom It is always easy to fit bodies of water into flat landscapes, as it is where we might expect to see them. In such a situation, marginal planting, where upright grassy species emerge from water, is very important for tying the pool into the surrounding landscape. In this design by Wolfgang Oehme and James van Sweden on Chesapeake Bay, the dominant flowering species is *Aster oblongifolius*.

Above The walls of ruins or rocks leading down to water are a rare opportunity that must be exploited to the full. In this garden by Dan Pearson, bold clumps of *Iris pseudacorus* stand out of the water; wisteria and roses drape the walls behind.

providing ready material for a landform. The trick is to disguise the fact that the landform is simply a convenient way of dumping the spoil. It must appear to be something in its own right, and make some kind of statement; a test would be to consider what it would look like if the water were not there.

This highlights the real difference in the degree to which landforms and water can or should be given a context. It needs to be made obvious that a landform is artificial, or it may be assumed that it is just a particularly knobbly part of the surroundings, or, even worse, that it has been left over by a less than competent landscaping team. Water, at least in the natural-style garden, should be convincingly sited and integrated. Even if we know a pond is artificial, the fact that it *could* have formed there naturally is part of the conceit. Water collects in the lowest areas, so it is clear that a pond should be made in the lowest part of the garden visible from the position where it is most likely to be seen. There are few things less convincing in a garden than a pond sited on a slope with an obvious bank around it holding the water in.

A pond is the most common form of water in a garden. It may work as a sculptural intervention in a landscape, but unplanted it looks bare; for the majority of us, the temptation to add a waterlily or a clump of reeds or irises at the edge soon becomes overwhelming.

Given the widely recognized importance of garden ponds for biodiversity, it is perhaps just as well that this is the case.

Few things are more useful for giving context to water than wetland-type planting, using the kind of plants that might be expected by a natural pond or in marshy country. Indeed, it is quite remarkable how such planting can help ease artificial ponds into a landscape or a garden. Waterside vegetation tends to be lush, and most of us make the subconscious link between tall, reedy grasses, big, fresh-green leaves or dense tussocks of sedges and the kind of plants we are familiar with from wild, wet places. Waterside or marginal vegetation is also valuable for wildlife; indeed, it is essential if a pond is to make a real impact on biodiversity. Much

Left Masses of reeds and long grass create a context for this large pond in a Northamptonshire garden by Dan Pearson. The largely wild native planting conveys a sense of calm.

Opposite, left Bold clumps of marginal planting, such as this *Iris pseudacorus* at the Clock House in Oxfordshire, link pond and surroundings. Such large species as this will need managing, however, as they can rapidly turn shallow pools into swamp rather than open water.

Opposite, right The landscape visible here varies between open water, unmown grass and, in the distance, mown grass. Rough grass helps create a romantic country atmosphere, whereas mown grass meeting water inevitably looks tame, or even suburban. This garden is by Julie Toll.

wildlife, from insect to mammal, will approach water only if it can do so under cover.

Wetland vegetation forms part of the gradation from dry to wet habitats typical of naturally occurring water. Many garden ponds, though, are constructed so that there is a sharp boundary between water and dry land. Fortunately, there are a great many garden plants that either are wetland species happy to grow in ordinary garden conditions, or are not actually wetland plants but look the part, and complete the illusion of wetland. Many of these are grasses or their relatives, the sedges, with lush, strap-like leaves, big, reed-like seed heads or tussocky habits of growth. Willows, too, are popularly associated with water. They do not *need* wet conditions; they just happen to grow near water because they can

survive there better than most other trees. Their presence, however, will be associated with moist soil, and so will help create the convincing fringe of vegetation that always accompanies natural pools.

Key to success in making water gardens and associated wetland areas is taking account of varying water levels – either the depth of actual water or the degree of waterlogging in the soil – since plants differ in their requirements. Aquatic plants themselves may be categorized according to whether they are free-floating, submerged or, like waterlilies (*Nymphaea* and *Nuphar* species), rooted in the bottom. Marginal plants grow at the edges or in shallow water, and vary in the depth of water they will tolerate. Bog plants are happy to grow in more or less permanently saturated soil. Those that like damp soil but will not thrive if kept constantly wet are often referred to as moisture-loving plants.

A pond and its fringe of planting, with different species of grasses, sedges and flowering plants forming successive bands according to their moisture requirements, is a good illustration of the way in which nature forms the sort of gradated sequence I have described above (see page 20). Getting this right is the best way to make a garden pond really feel like a

Opposite The pond here acts as a foreground focal point, between the trim mown lawn of the garden (by John Brookes) and the rural landscape beyond. Without the marginal planting it would look very bare.

Right, top There is nothing like waterside trees to make a pond look established. Fortunately, most grow very fast. Occasionally mown grass, rather than tight-cropped lawn, around the water helps to maintain a natural atmosphere. Dead logs half in, half out of the water are a good wildlife habitat and are much appreciated as roosting places for ducks. This planting is by John Brookes.

Right, bottom Ponds in urban gardens are inevitably restricted when it comes to tying in with their surroundings. This one in a Hertfordshire garden by Julie Toll cleverly uses common native waterside plants as its backdrop, including magenta *Lythrum salicaria* and *Filipendula ulmaria*.

piece of nature. It is also important in ecological terms. Particular plant species tend to colonize a certain part of a moisture gradient because that is where they grow and compete best, and the different habitats they create will also attract different invertebrates, so each gradation will tend to develop its own distinctive ecosystem.

There is one big and very important subject associated with planting in the wet: that of plant size. Water and wetland plants tend to grow fast, and often form very large colonies of only one species. Far too often, plants are innocently put in at the edge of a pond, and within a couple of years the entire pool is choked with vegetation, more often than not that of just one species. This is all the more common with natural-style pools, simply because more plants are likely to be used, and such rapid growth will be welcomed at first. Removal of such invasive plants can be a major task.

Selecting the right plants can greatly reduce the long-term problem of managing plants that are too big for the site. You need to do your research, especially if the pond is small or shallow, and make sure you choose plants of an appropriate size. As an example, consider the reedmaces – the genus *Typha*. *Typha latifolia*, the common reedmace, is widespread across the northern hemisphere, and its distinctive chestnut-brown cylindrical seed heads are one of the iconic sights of natural waterside environments. This being so, it is very tempting to plant it if you are seeking inspiration from nature. But plant this thug in anything other than a very large pool, with water deeper than 60 cm (2 ft), and in no time at all there will be no water visible – only a solid mass of these rushes. *T. angustifolia* is smaller, growing in water up to 30 cm (1 ft) deep, but still too vigorous for anything other than larger garden ponds. There is, however, a variegated form, *T. latifolia* 'Variegata', which is smaller and less vigorous. For the really small pond, even a mini-pond in a container on a terrace, *T. minima* is the ideal plant,

needing only 5 cm (2 in) of water in which to grow, and reaching a height of only 50 cm (1 ft 8 in).

There are good ecological reasons for the large size of so many water and bog plants: resources (water and nutrients) are plentiful, so plants will compete for them, and in the plant competition stakes, the biggest and most vigorous wins. Water and bog plants suitable for small pools are not so common, and may need to be sought out from specialist nurseries. The large size and vigorous growth of water plants mean that they are also more likely to become a problem if they escape from the garden and enter the wild; many of the worst problems some countries have experienced with non-native exotics have involved waterside or wetland plants. A good example is purple loosestrife (*Lythrum salicaria*), which is native to

Europe but has run rampant in North American wetlands. It is always advisable to use only regionally native species when planting up streams or ditches connected to a river system, otherwise what you grow in your garden may end up multiplying far downstream.

That wetland is a competitive environment goes some way towards explaining why the wetland year tends to be later than the year on dry land. Dry-habitat plants need to flower and produce seed before the sun dries out the ground, but in wet locations, flowering too early wastes resources that might be better spent on fighting for space through the production of leaves and stems. Early-flowering wetland plants tend to flower *very* early (species of *Caltha*, for example, and the dramatic arum lily relative, species of *Lysichiton*), well before the extensive growth of other plants.

Opposite Even the most rigidly formal pool may be given some life with marginal planting, such as these *Schoenoplectus* rushes planted by Dan Pearson. Plants for such locations can be grown in pots, which makes installing them easy. It is important that the right plant is chosen for the particular depth of water.

Above Marginal planting here by John Brookes fulfils a number of functions: it helps provide a foreground for the water, itself a division between the more intimate area of the garden and the less-managed part behind, and it creates a barrier in front of the water.

Most flower only once they have extended their leaves, and quite a few delay flowering until well after midsummer.

Flowers are in any case often rather overwhelmed in wetland habitats by the sheer dominance of lush green foliage. It is this foliage that is the chief joy of garden wetlands, and design considerations should really start with an attempt to celebrate the variety and luxuriance of the wide range of water-loving plants available. The dominant leaf shape in natural wetlands is the linear thrust of such plants as reeds, rushes, reedmace and irises: plants that often occupy large monocultural expanses. In trying to create a natural look in the garden it is well to remember this linear dominance. Another shape, less common but highly distinctive, is the broad umbrella, which may be vast – as in the case of the giant rhubarb relative *Gunnera manicata* – or simply big, as in *Astilboides tabularis*. This broad shape may appear as palmate (hand-shaped), as in rodgersias. Smaller leaves than these giants are

Left This pool is surrounded by some particularly lush planting by Dan Pearson. From left to right: *Iris versicolor, Caltha palustris* (which has deep-yellow flowers in early spring) and *Ligularia stenocephala*. The first two grow naturally in the almost permanently waterlogged soil around water; the last is more typical of seasonally wet ground.

Above *Iris versicolor* is one of several irises that thrive in either very wet soil or shallow water. They have a tendency to form single-species blocks, as do a great many marginal or wetland plants. The plume-like flower heads of a rodgersia are just visible on the left of this planting, which is also by Dan Pearson.

often still large and lush compared with those of related non-wetland species.

Managing the boundary between water and dry land is key to the overall visual success of water in the garden. Conventional stone edgings have tended to give way to a fashion for pebble beaches, a conceit that does not necessarily work, and can look very out of place somewhere far from the sea or a river. Mown grass leading down to the water can look suburban, at least if more than a small proportion of the frontage is so treated. A truly natural-looking alternative, a thick boundary of marginal plants or shrubs, would have the effect of making the water inaccessible (although this does have the virtue of making it very difficult for young children to fall in, rendering unattractive barriers unnecessary). One of the most popular solutions is decking or boardwalks (which are really simply linear decking). They work very well with water because they hide the

Opposite, left *Petasites japonicus* var. *giganteus*, on the left, is a dramatic, rapidly spreading perennial suitable for extensive waterside locations. To the back are the white plumes of *Aruncus dioicus*, a tall, bulky perennial that thrives in shade. This is the Hannah Peschar Sculpture Garden, Surrey, by Anthony Paul.

Opposite, right The *Rodgersia podophylla* dominating here in Mount Usher Gardens, County Wicklow, Ireland, is one of many plants that like damp soil, but perform best on wet slopes or beside streams rather than with their roots permanently waterlogged. Damp, but only rarely wet, soil is the next best situation. Except at high latitudes, rodgersias tend to do best in shade; hot sun burns their magnificent bronze–green foliage.

Above *Gunnera manicata*, seen here at Derrynane House, County Kerry, Ireland, is the most majestic of waterside plants. *G. tinctoria* is similar but smaller. Gunneras are slow to reach full size.

water's edge, creating the illusion of hovering above its surface. Decking that projects over a pond or stream, in particular, allows observation of deeper water, not just the shallows. An attractive answer is to opt for a stretch of decking and use marginal planting for the remainder.

Finally, it is worth considering trees and shrubs when looking at how to make a water garden seem realistic and function naturally. Trees or large shrubs around water are particularly important for bird habitats. Natural stretches of water are often surrounded by trees that are distinctive of wet habitats, such as alders (*Alnus*), willows (*Salix*) and poplars (*Populus*). Many are simply too large for domestic gardens, but some, especially willows, may be kept small by coppicing (see page 76). When the plant has highly coloured young stems, as do many willows and dogwoods, coppicing is a good way of ensuring that there is a renewed display each spring. Coppicing and its related technique, pollarding, create distinctive shapes that are typical of many traditional wetland areas, and the straight rods of new growth they generate are also very useful in the garden (see 'Sculpture and Ornament', above).

Opposite and above The simplest bridge – although not one recommended for crossing deep water – is the unpretentious plank type with no sides. Unlike those more solidly constructed with parapets, such bridges look impermanent and rustic, which increases the (probably false) impression that they are hardly ever used or are somewhere out in the wilderness. These bridges are in gardens by John Brookes (*opposite, top*), Julie Toll (*opposite, bottom*) and Jinny Blom (*above*).

Left Staggered bridges of this kind are associated with Japanese gardens, where they originated as a means of encouraging the user to pay attention to their surroundings. This one is at the Hannah Peschar Sculpture Garden in Surrey, by Anthony Paul.

140

Plants for Water Gardens

Below, left Gunnera tinctoria, a giant rhubarb relative, behind the circular leaves of *Darmera peltata*. Both plants are species of the water's edge, not immersed but with their crowns just above the water. The darmera in particular is good for holding together muddy banks, as its rhizomes spread out over the surface of the soil.

Below, right Species and hybrids of miscanthus are among the best plants for planting in the moist ground near water, as they look just enough like reeds to remind us of these waterside grasses, but without having their invasive habits. They will also thrive in ordinary garden soil.

Opposite, top left The Japanese species *Iris ensata* is extremely showy, but particular: it needs lime-free soil and likes plenty of water in the summer, but dislikes being waterlogged in the winter.

Opposite, bottom left A rodgersia with the ostrich fern (*Matteuccia struthiopteris*) in the background. Both are plants of damp ground, preferably in light shade. If they grow well, rodgersias are among the most majestic foliage plants for moist places.

Opposite, right Waterlilies (species and hybrids of *Nymphaea* and *Nuphar*) are the quintessential aquatic plants. In this example of a traditional formal pond they illustrate their value as good creators of habitat, creating shade beneath their leaves.

Gunnera tinctoria

Miscanthus sp.

Iris ensata

Rodgersia sp. and Matteuccia struthiopteris

Nymphaea sp.

Gardens and the Wider Landscape

A GARDEN INEVITABLY FORMS PART OF ITS landscape. In some instances the surroundings dominate overwhelmingly and the task of the garden-maker is to allow the garden to exist as an entity in its own right – as is the case with many small urban gardens. In others, particularly in rural areas, the garden might appear to be an intimate part of the wider landscape, and anything done in it might therefore have a considerable impact on its local environment. It is this relationship between garden and rural surroundings that I examine here. A natural-style garden in the country should be in harmony with its setting. That is not to say it has to look like its surroundings or be indistinguishable from them, but rather it should acknowledge and respect them. Here, I will look at the subject of relating gardens to landscapes, and in particular at how a naturalistic planting style can help create a sense of a garden belonging to its locality and a zone of transition between the two.

Many involved with gardening care deeply about landscapes, and especially about those in the countryside. We want to protect them and yet make our own essentially selfish and anthropocentric interventions – which are at the core of the creativity that makes gardening an art form. At the same time, we must recognize that nearly all European landscapes, and a great many elsewhere, are the result of human intervention, of centuries or even millennia of clearing, cultivation and management. There is clearly a big contradiction here: between artistic creativity, which is a large part of what makes us human, and our desire to preserve and conserve. This mirrors the private world of the garden and the public world of the landscape.

Anyone who has ever worked in a garden centre knows when a particular plant has been featured on a gardening television programme from the refrain of enquiries the following weekend. The fact that everyone is after the same plants illustrates how gardening is a hobby that operates on a nation- or region-wide basis, and

Previous page Houses and gardens may be immersed completely in their surroundings, as in this garden by Tom Vanderpoel in Wisconsin. This is clearly the best way to minimize the property's impact on the environment, but is perhaps not to everyone's taste.

Above Views from windows are crucial to the enjoyment of many gardens, and of the surroundings. The extent to which such views should attempt to blur the boundary between garden and wider landscape is a matter of taste, but most gardeners would seek to achieve a sense of their garden belonging to its locale. This house and garden were designed by Jean Kling.

Right This garden by Jinny Blom is an oasis of cultivation in an area of great natural beauty. Surrounded by deciduous woodland, it blends into its environment: there are no evergreens or trees with coloured foliage to disrupt the view. The use of areas of native wild flowers helps to create a link with the countryside, too.

Gardens in areas where rocks or other strong natural features make themselves felt are often interesting and well integrated with their surroundings. The sheer intractability of such environments can force a compromise between nature and garden-making. Minimal interventions can be the best way to create garden spaces, respecting the geology and the natural plant communities that grow there. At Torrecchia in Italy, Dan Pearson created a mown grass path and left everything 'natural' on either side.

how gardeners are increasingly planting the same species. In some cases the plants that are becoming popular are exotic-looking species from far-flung parts of the globe.

There could be a problem here. Do we want all our gardens to look the same, with no sense of regional diversity, or any sense that planting must relate to its surroundings? Those characteristics that make certain plants so popular in the garden can also make them stand out from their surroundings, drawing attention not only to themselves but also to the fact that here, yet again, is the hand of twenty-first-century humanity. The problem is perhaps at its worst when highly distinctive trees that bear no relation to native species – or indeed any naturally occurring species whatsoever – are grown in areas of traditional rural landscape; those with yellow foliage, such as many cypresses and *Robinia pseudoacacia* 'Frisia', in particular, can be seen from considerable distances.

But don't gardeners have a right to grow what they like? Don't we all have freedom of horticultural expression? Where do we draw the boundaries? Perhaps the best way to strike a balance is to think in terms of those gradations described on page 20. I think we need to look first at the greater or lesser extent to which plants fit into rural, semi-natural landscapes, and secondly at the impact gardens may have on their surroundings.

Gardens can be hidden from their surroundings or visible from far away. The extent of this visibility is a good guide to how we choose what to grow. Gardens in urban areas or which are screened from their surroundings are clearly the concern of the owner and no one else, but the greater the visibility of the garden the greater needs to be the care with which those who plant trees or 'attention-seeking' plants think about how they will be seen. At the far end of the spectrum is the garden in a prominent position in an area of great natural beauty.

Locally native plants clearly belong anywhere the habitat suits them. Perennials and most shrubs soon disappear into the background, and so are not a problem. In addition, a great many hardy, non-native garden plants have a similar habit and colouring, to the extent that virtually everyone will simply overlook the fact that many deciduous trees of American origin are 'alien' to a European landscape, and many Chinese ones are not native to American surroundings. Conifers and evergreens, however, will certainly stand out in areas where they are not found naturally, or where there has been no history of planting them. Similarly, there is a good case for saying that trees with prominent yellow or variegated foliage should not be grown in areas of traditional or 'unspoiled' rural beauty, as they can be seen from so far away. Finally, those species that look dramatically different from native plants and tend immediately to seize the attention, such as palms and yuccas in cool temperate zones, need perhaps to be restricted to where they do not impinge on rural landscapes.

Perhaps the key is sensitivity. Gardeners and designers need to develop an awareness of their surroundings and a sensitivity to what is appropriate, and to remember that in rural areas or built environments with a traditional character, the important idea is perhaps not to 'contrast' but to 'complement'.

The concept of 'borrowed landscape' is one that has been highly developed in Japan's sophisticated garden culture. In the Western tradition the emphasis has tended to be on creating places in the garden where particularly spectacular views can be appreciated: using the wider scenic landscape as theatrical backdrop for the garden's stage, if you like. The Japanese approach has been more subtle, taking a feature of the outside landscape – perhaps a craggy hilltop or an attractive grove of trees – and making it part of the garden by framing it with trees or shrubs. The landscape is captured as a picture or view from a window. The slow way to do this is by planting; the quick way is

Below Native flora can be used to create links with the locale of a garden. Here, in a garden by Ted Smyth in New Zealand, species of *Carex* help root aggressively contemporary architecture into its environment.

Right This example of 'modernist formality', by Piet Oudolf, uses a common native grass of northern Europe, *Deschampsia cespitosa*, in blocks. The grass species itself evokes natural habitats, while the geometry echoes the straight lines of the canals and the field shapes of the cultivated landscape of Holland. The loosely pruned hedge on the left combines native with non-native species, making an informal and effective screen, although its size and billowing shapes are not typical for traditional utilitarian country hedges. The space is designed by Piet Boon.

by judicious trimming of branches or felling in order
to reveal glimpses of the surroundings.

Trees, as the elements in the garden most visible
from outside and the most dominating of space within,
play a crucial role in a garden's relationship with the
external landscape. In urban areas the use of native trees
may be only a symbolic reference to a natural landscape
that is no longer there; in rural areas it will meld the
garden with the landscape. From the outside, trees
can hide the garden and the house or make it feel part
of the landscape. From the inside, they can help the
whole garden blend into the surroundings. This can
be achieved either by planting within the garden or by
creating a boundary screen that brings the landscape in.

Boundary hedges can play a crucial role in relating
a garden to its landscape. Hedges are conventionally
separated into two kinds: formal – kept clipped and
relatively geometric – and informal – loose and free-
growing – with the latter usually interpreted as being the
more 'natural'. More interesting, however, is the creation
of mixed hedges, based on a combination of species

Right, top Deciduous trees will
always link a garden with a
landscape where deciduous
species predominate, no matter
what their geographic origin.
These maples at The Homewood
in Surrey have at some stage had
lower branches removed, giving
a high canopy and minimizing
the shade cast beneath them.

Right, bottom It is simply
impossible to tell where this
garden (also The Homewood
in Surrey) ends – a visual trick
achieved through the planting
of trees.

Opposite, left A geometric, and very
unnaturalistic, garden by Graham
Pockett has a backdrop of trees
that provides a natural-looking
way of linking the garden with
the wider landscape. Their height
ensures that they will always
dominate the garden, and their
shapes and textures balance the
garden's hard lines.

Opposite, right This garden by Pietro
Porcinai is inevitably dominated
by the woodland surrounding
it. Its wall ensures that it is
perceived as a very separate
place, but the climbers subtly
minimize the wall's impact,
making the garden feel very
much part of its surroundings.

traditionally used as country hedges to edge fields. These are conventionally cut in a somewhat crudely geometric way, although historically they have been 'laid': a very skilled technique of partially cutting stems and trunks, and bending them over to form horizontals, which mesh together to form an animal-proof barrier. Such a procedure may be unnecessary in a suburban garden, but it creates an evocation of country life that many find attractive.

The use of a mix of hedging species creates interest, and is particularly useful for spreading that interest across the seasons. A variety is also potentially of great wildlife value – another example of floristic diversity supporting a wider biodiversity.

Trees and shrubs may be the most obvious way of blurring boundaries between the garden and its rural surroundings, but there are others, too. Rustic fences or drystone walls are more typical of traditional utilitarian barriers in country areas, and are therefore better at creating subtle garden boundaries. One particular type relies on eliminating an impression of boundary altogether, and has a name originating in an eighteenth-century English landowner's joke: the 'ha-ha'. The ditch is,

Opposite, top left Beds of ornamental grasses form part of the boundary between this garden by Jean Kling and the agricultural landscape beyond. Even when not in flower or seed, the clearly defined clumps of most such species are a distinctive feature.

Opposite, top right A view of one kind of ha-ha, in which a fence serves as the barrier, and the steep bank (on the left) is higher than the top of the fence, concealing it from view. The garden is by Dan Pearson, in Warwickshire.

Opposite, bottom left Ornamental grasses forming a transition zone in the same garden by Dan Pearson. *Stipa gigantea* is big enough to be dramatic, but has a very similar overall appearance to wild species. Grasses from a wide range of regions share basic characteristics, making them very suitable for naturalistic planting.

Opposite, bottom right A lawn merges into a pastoral landscape, as mown grass gives way to unmown. Again, this is by Dan Pearson in Warwickshire.

Above A bank of meadow grasses and wild flowers brings the countryside into this garden by Jinny Blom, integrating it with its surroundings. The white flower is ox-eye daisy, *Leucanthemum vulgare*, a short-lived species of dry meadows. Ox-eyes are an example of what is known as a 'pioneer' species: one that grows rapidly on a new site and then dies out unless new sites for its seedlings become available. As the grasses and slower-growing wild flowers in the mix become established, the room for ox-eye seedlings is reduced.

in fact, one of the earliest forms of large-scale boundary marker, and a ditch with a fence running along the bottom serves as an animal-proof boundary (as does a ditch with a very steep, high drop on the side nearest the land it is protecting). The beauty of the ha-ha is that, in a grassland landscape, there is no obvious break in the ground when seen from more than a few strides away. Thus, taking to an extreme the concept of borrowed landscape, the entire view merges with the garden.

Ha-has are associated with large, estate-type gardens, but they can also work very well in smaller gardens. A short stretch between boundary shrubs can beautifully frame distant views and create a wonderful sense of illusion. The only drawback, apart from the

effort required to dig it out, is that the wall on the garden side is faced with a slope of relatively shallow gradient, which needs to be several metres wide.

Grasses, by the very fact that they tend to dominate open habitats, and in particular pastoral landscapes, can play an important role in blurring garden boundaries. Traditionally, gardens have tended to be seen as a series of concentric circles, with the most formal and highly managed areas nearest the house and wilder areas further away. This idea is easily extended to grass or lawn management, with regularly mown lawn giving way to infrequently mown, longer grass in the outer reaches. Just how this is achieved will depend to some extent on how the grass develops once mowing is reduced, particularly on fertile soils. Unmown grass (even what was once fine lawn grass) tends to become dominated by tussocky and rather rank-looking pasture grasses. However, occasional mowing – at least once a year – will stop this happening. An alternative is to treat the outer reaches of the lawn as a 'moving boundary' and mow the area perhaps for just part of the year (which works very well with naturalized daffodils), or mow it in patterns, changing the pattern every year. One of the best means of following this practice is to mow paths through the grass for at least part of the summer.

In regions where bunch grasses are common (see pages 41–42), simply mowing will not tame the tussocky grasses. It is far better to live with them, control any aggressive weeds that appear, and try to add some interesting wild flowers. They are part of the hand

Left Rustic fences are a good way of making divisions that maintain the feeling that the garden continues beyond.

Opposite A border of lush planting, including many cottage garden plants, such as hollyhocks (*Alcea*) and lilies (*Lilium*), creates a background that merges so effectively with the green of the trees and shrubs behind that it is not at all obvious where this small garden (Jinny Blom's own) actually ends.

nature has dealt you, and as such are part of the scenery. Most ornamental grasses are bunch-forming species, and they can be used to create interesting zones of transition between landscape and garden. Many do undeniably look different from the species to be found around many rural gardens, but they rarely look out of place, and, most importantly, their subtle colouring will ensure that they do not obtrude too deeply into the surroundings.

Any reasonably wild-looking planting can be used to create soft boundary zones. The key elements are plants that look as though they could be found growing wild nearby, even though they may not be locally native. Shrubs are often the right size to act as a screen. Whereas lines of shrubs tend to look suspiciously like a hedge, staggering the planting locations and adding random 'outliers' makes for a much more accidental-looking boundary. Underplanting shrubs with perennials, or a mixture of wild grasses and wild flowers, and extending this as an apron also creates a naturalistic boundary.

Opposite, top left and bottom Infinity pools are an elegant way of creating boundaries. The lower image shows a swimming pool, forming a visual and physical boundary at the edge of a steep drop in a garden by Karena Batstone. The pool in the top image, on the other hand, has been designed specifically as an alternative to a fence or wall, either of which would have interrupted the view. The garden is by Isabelle Greene.

Opposite, top right Very clearly acting as a boundary, this pool by Steve Martino in Tucson, Arizona, is almost surreal in its juxtaposition with a desert landscape. The reflection of the sculptural forms of desert plants in its still surface subtly connects it with its surroundings.

Right, top The view over water from Niall McLaughlin's Shack in Northamptonshire can only be described as dramatic. With decking as the boundary between house and water, the relationship between the two becomes immediate. A thick growth of willows ensures that the whole property is immersed in its landscape.

Right, bottom Swimming pools, with their intense colour and concrete surrounds, are notoriously difficult to hide. In both these cases, trees and shrubs screen them as much as possible from their surroundings. The left-hand garden is by Jinny Blom; the right-hand one by Luis Vallejo.

Water and wetlands can make very effective boundaries. There is a certain ambiguity about a pond: it may very clearly separate what lies on either side, but by not being an obvious line like a fence or hedge it successfully disguises the actual boundary. Wetlands, where there are luxuriant moisture-loving plants but no open water, are even more ambiguous, and can create particularly subtle transition effects.

Water, for many gardeners, is the habitat where the complexity and dynamism of life (insect, bird and amphibian, as well as plant) is most apparent. Linking wetland and water is often the best way to contextualize water bodies and make them look natural, as well as the best way to support burgeoning biodiversity. Indeed, many see their ponds as the focal point of their gardens.

Above It is not a conventional hedge, but this line of espalier-trained apple trees, underplanted with loosely pruned box, serves to divide one part of this garden by Jinny Blom from another.

Right A wetland can be effective as an invisible boundary. The purple flowers in this planting by John Brookes are purple loosestrife (*Lythrum salicaria*), a European species that has become invasive in North America, and consequently is illegal to plant in many states. Many of the worst invasive plant problems concern species of wetland habitats, so gardeners need to be very cautious about planting vigorous species in places where wetland or open water is connected to local waterways.

Sun and Stone

SUN AND STONE ARE NATURAL PARTNERS. STONE in shade or damp places soon discolours; in sun it retains its untarnished, raw appearance for much longer. Stone in dry climates is unlikely to be covered or concealed by vegetation, so it makes its presence felt much more in the landscape at every level, from the widest vista to the smallest garden nook. In damper climates, stone is not naturally so visible, let alone dominant, unless it is a mountain region. Where stone may not be part of the norm, its appearance in the garden is more of a special event, perhaps one that is all the more special because it will not last long unchanged.

That stone is the very substance of the earth itself daily confronts those in mountainous or hilly dry regions, but is all too easily forgotten by those in lush lowlands. Stone has a solidity and weight, not just physically but visually, and that is one reason for its popularity with gardeners. Its sheer usefulness in the garden can all too easily blind us to its appearance, however, and to some of its disadvantages. Given that the presence and availability of stone varies so greatly from one place to another, it is crucial to bear in mind the extent to which stone is *naturally* part of a garden or environment.

As in drier climates stone is less likely to be covered in vegetation, so its relationship with the sun becomes more prominent. Sunlight is also necessary for us to appreciate the subtleties of stone: its shape, texture and colour. Just how much sun and stone we want is a personal matter, however. Too much of this powerful

Previous page Stone found during construction has been used to build an embankment in this California garden by Isabelle Greene. Unshaped and unadorned by cosmetic improvement, this stone has a raw energy about it, helping to meld the house and its terrace into the landscape. The plants selected are all sun-loving and drought-tolerant species, but their roots will be able to penetrate deep into the soil at the sides of the rock for coolness and moisture. Their low, sprawling shape is common in drought-tolerant plants.

Opposite, top A feathergrass, *Stipa capillata*, makes a brief impact in a planting on a dry, stony soil in Jinny Blom's own garden. Many of the most attractive ornamental grasses are natives of such habitats. To the left are California poppies, *Eschscholzia californica*, a self-sowing annual, and at the rear are the white flower spikes of a verbascum; both groups of plants are happy in dry habitats.

Opposite, bottom Dry, stony soils may seem difficult environments, but they do support a very attractive wild flora, albeit one with a relatively short season of interest (generally spring to early summer in temperate and Mediterranean-type climates). In this planting by Dan Pearson, varieties of *Eremurus* provide a spectacular forest of flower spikes. The purple is *Salvia* × *sylvestris* 'Mainacht'. The selection of drought-tolerant species for such habitats is key to minimizing irrigation.

Right Space for a house is hewn out of the bedrock. It looks almost disturbingly raw, but in time it will weather and plants will grow over enough of the surface to make it look like a natural outcrop. Some may find this a scar on the landscape, but its long-term development will ensure that this approach is visually preferable to and more sustainable than the alternative: the erection of a concrete retaining wall. Rock, almost by definition, belongs to a landscape; concrete will always be alien to it. This Californian garden is designed by Isabelle Greene.

combination may overwhelm, particularly in climates or places that are dry and exposed for much of the year; the reaction of many people in such places is to feel that the sun is relentless and merciless, and what they seek is shade and cool, moist air. But for those who want to celebrate this most natural combination, who want to be like lizards, which need to bask in the sun before they have enough energy to live and perform, may see the combination of sun and stone as being at the core of what they want in the garden.

Stone soaks up the warmth of the sun, but loses it rapidly at night, so plants growing around it experience a microclimate different from elsewhere in the garden – hotter and drier, but subject to greater extremes of temperature. This may be a problem where the sun is strong and water short, but not if the right plants are chosen. The heating and cooling effect has even been exploited by gardeners in humid climates to cultivate plants from arid regions in gravel or stone gardens. Those in situations where sun and stone dominate should be among the first to recognize the importance of the 'right plant, right place' philosophy. However, there is a counter-intuitive side to stone in the garden: at depth, stone protects the soil from the sun's heat, and water often condenses on its cool lower surfaces during the night. That is why farmers across the Middle East pile stones around the bases of trees. The cool, moist underground surfaces of stones can be a lifeline for plants growing around them.

Stone takes many forms in a garden. A primary distinction is between bedrock (or stone derived from local bedrock) and stone that has been imported from a geologically different region. The exposure of bedrock is the exposure of the very earth itself, so a garden built around bedrock is likely to be dominated by it, a reminder of just how thin the layer of life is on planet Earth. Even where bedrock is deeply buried, it may

Left, top Large expanses of stone may have spaces for creating niches. These are an attractive option for soft stone, and make good display places for pots. This one is in Judy and David Drew's own garden in France.

Left, bottom Rockfaces, especially those of easily worked stone, were sometimes used by traditional agricultural societies for making storage cellars and even houses. Now, they are left as enigmatic reminders of times past. Such places nearly always look best as semi-ruins, unadorned by attempts at beautification or design.

Opposite The three forms in which stone is customarily used in gardens come together in this design by Luis Vallejo: natural, cut and as gravel. Ideally, they should all be derived from the same type of stone, or at least be of similar colour and texture; remember that often-repeated design motto, 'less is more'. Natural rocks with several decades, or even centuries, of weathering and a flora of lichens and moss are valuable finds for garden use. Contrast with raw, unweathered surfaces should be avoided if at all possible.

dominate a landscape if it has been traditionally used for building. So, either through exposure or construction, stone derived from local bedrock is a reminder of the area's geology. The consequence of this is that to use local stone in a garden is to make a link with the locality, with both its geology and its history.

Stone imported from another area may often seem out of place or artificial, but there will be no alternative if there is no local source. Increasingly, however, garden stone is being transported over huge distances, so there is often the absurd situation in which it is cheaper in Europe or North America to buy stone that has been shipped from India or China. There are clearly issues of environmental transport costs here! Human rights must also be a consideration: quarrying in some countries is carried out by bonded labour, a form of slavery. Perhaps more so than for any other commodity, it is important that stone should be sourced reasonably locally.

Understanding the origins of stone and how it relates to landscape is an important part of learning how to use it properly. There are three basic categories: igneous, sedimentary and metamorphic. Igneous rock is of volcanic origin; it may, like basalt, originate as lava, or, like granite, well up from deep within the earth and

Stone flags are used in this garden by Dan Pearson to create a transition zone between a border running along the foundations of the house and the lawn. Gaps have been left in the paving in order to allow planting to continue the theme of the border. Plants for such a location need to be chosen carefully. Low-growing species with large basal leaves are particularly successful: silver *Stachys byzantina* and the rounded green foliage of *Alchemilla mollis* are two important elements here. The mauve–blue scattered along the length of the border is *Perovskia atriplicifolia*, valuable for its midsummer flowering and tolerance of hot, dry conditions (and bitterly cold winters).

Opposite, left Red valerian, *Centranthus ruber*, grows along the foot of a border spilling out over a path of stone flags, in Piet Oudolf's garden for Bury Court in Hampshire. While growing in a conventional border here, this is a species that thrives in much drier situations, even growing in old stone walls. The grass on the left is *Stipa gigantea*. Achieving the right width for a path running through planting is a crucial decision: too narrow and plants spilling over the edges will impede access and soak users

in wet weather; too wide and the sense of intimacy disappears. It helps, when making such a decision, to know to what extent neighbouring plants will spill over.

Opposite, right A path of stone setts runs between borders of naturalistic planting by Jinny Blom. Some moss and grass has begun to grow in the gaps between the setts, creating a sense of connection with the lush, green surroundings. The white flowers are *Leucanthemum vulgare*.

become exposed millions of years later as the upper layers of rock are eroded. Sedimentary rocks are laid down layer by layer, usually under water, becoming steadily more compressed, before being lifted up to form dry land again: sandstones are derived from sand deposits, shales from finer, clay-like particles, and limestones from the remains of vast numbers of tiny sea-creatures with hard, calcareous body parts. Metamorphic stone is the result of heat and pressure changing the nature of pre-existing rocks.

Sedimentary rocks are set apart by the layering effect created by their slow process of accumulation. Their

layers (technically called strata) make them easy to
work, which is why some make such good paving slabs
and others good building materials; they are also an
important part of the stone's appearance. Like the grain
in wood, the layers in rock often dictate how the material
can be used. Igneous rocks generally have no such grain,
which in many ways makes them more difficult to use;
they often have a characteristically lumpy appearance.
Some, notably granites, may have a distinctive
appearance resulting from the size and range of crystals
of which they are composed. Metamorphic rocks are a
varied bunch: marbles may be spectacular when cut and
polished, but as raw stone tend to be formless and dull;
slates, however, are one of the most exciting stones to
use in the garden, with their dark colour and the ease
with which they can be made into thin slabs.

There is also a kind of visual synergy about stone,
of which gardeners need to be aware. Regions where
sedimentary rocks predominate tend to be gentle lowlands,
so the strata of the stone can seem to reflect the layering

Left To what extent different
rock types can be juxtaposed
is subjective. In this garden by
Isabelle Greene, the pale gravel
emphasizes the rich colour and
texture of the slate. It is also
worth noting that the slate
includes a secondary colour,
which is almost identical to
that of the gravel.

Opposite, top left A striking
combination of gravel and slate
by Luis Vallejo. Slate is extremely
useful for paths but can become
slippery in humid climates.

Opposite, right Paths of stone setts
sweep and curve between lush
herbaceous borders in Piet
Oudolf's garden at Bury Court,
Hampshire. Several of the plant

clumps close to the path have
a rounded shape, echoing the
curves of the path. During
the growing season the paths'
progress becomes partly
concealed behind planting,
creating a sense of mystery about
where they are to go. One of the
advantages of curving paths, as
opposed to straight, is that there
is always uncertainty in the mind
about their destination. During
the winter, once dead plant
material has been cleared away,
their progress is much clearer
and they serve as an architectural
feature in their own right. Note
the definite curve, or camber, in
the cross-section of the path;
this serves to drain water away
from the path's surface.

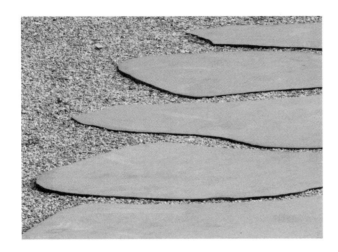

of the landscape. Country dominated by igneous and metamorphic rocks is more likely to be mountainous, hilly or have an unpredictable quality about it.

In many cases, most of the stone visible in a garden is in the house itself, or in associated buildings, or garden or boundary walls. Paving and gravel areas come second, while deliberate use of stone for its own sake tends to be small-scale, in Western cultures at any rate. China and Japan have a very different attitude to stone, and one that is much more sophisticated and nuanced. If a house is built of stone, and especially if that stone is also used in the garden, it will set a theme. Any additional use of stone must blend in.

Contrast between stone of different origins must be handled carefully. Too much contrast stands out very strongly, and using more than two types of stone in a garden is liable to make it feel like a geology museum. Contrast is read differently by different people, and anyone who knows anything about stone is likely to spot inconsistencies and find them irritating and jarring.

The colour of gravel and stone, especially in full sun, has a strong effect on the surroundings. Pale material, especially grey, highlights colour, making gravel

Left In stony regions, boundaries made from unmortared material – known as drystone walls – are common. Country gardens, such as this one by Lesley Rosser, may incorporate them. New walls may be built by local craftspeople – and it is not too difficult an art to learn. They are low enough to see over, a useful quality in gardens where a sense of division is needed but where there are views to be preserved.

Opposite Gravels of various colours are used in this Californian garden by Isabelle Greene to create a stream effect, somewhat reminiscent of Japanese gardens. Additional stones here are the same colour as the gravel forming the 'land', so enhancing the illusion. Gravel used in this way is particularly valuable for covering areas of concrete or other hard surfaces, where planting is impossible or difficult, but where the impression of natural forms is wanted. Keeping different-coloured gravels separate will be an important, and possibly time-consuming, maintenance task; for this reason such an area can be only looked at, and not walked on.

gardens ideal places in which to make the most of the hues of flowers and leaves. Red or pink stone tends to highlight green, making an effective contrast with foliage. Light stone in areas of strong sunlight may be dazzling, and grey stone in those where overcast skies are common, depressing. In both cases, planting has an important role to play in moderating the effect.

Stone comes in different forms: as blocks, as slabs or as gravel. Blocks may have a distinctive character of their own, although this depends on the nature of the rock, and indeed its history, as erosion or weathering may have had an influence on its shape. Those interested in natural-style gardening usually want to cut stone artificially as little as possible, so rock types that naturally split into slabs are extremely useful. Stone slabs are ideal for stepping-stone paths, and smaller ones for assembling into drystone walls, which may be freestanding or act as retaining walls. Stone that naturally splits into layers always does so unevenly, and in the process often reveals a surprising range of colours. This unevenness produces a natural appearance far removed from the regularity of artificially cut stone.

Gravels, preferably derived from local stone, have a great many uses in the garden. A gravel mulch is one of the most effective ways of reducing water loss from garden plants and suppressing the growth of weed seedlings. It also makes it possible to achieve a blurred transition between unplanted areas, such as paths and drives, and planted areas, as plants can be dotted around. Gravel instantly makes a garden look sun-baked and dry, even if it is not, so the planting must be appropriate: hummocky, grey-leaved shrubs, low, tussocky grasses, spiky rosette plants and any others that look as though they might have come from a dry hillside. There is a practical side to such choices, too: combine lush planting with gravel and every autumn there will be quantities of dead leaves, which, if not scrupulously

This excellent example of the wilder kind of gravel garden is by John Brookes, at Denmans Garden in West Sussex. A variety of stone sizes creates the illusion of a dry river bed. Plants are also being allowed to self-sow: the pink is foxglove, *Digitalis purpurea*, and the silver-leaved yellow *Verbascum bombyciferum*. Both are biennials, which means that plentiful seedlings can be expected in the gravel the year after flowering; an excess is easily removed. The clump of linear foliage with mauve flowers is *Iris versicolor*.

A classic gravel garden, where expanses of stone separate clusters of plants. Stepping stones provide an obvious route for access, but the gravel makes other routes possible and permissible. Two sizes of gravel are used, giving a richer visual experience and creating the illusion of a dry river bed. The yellow flower is an *Achillea millefolium* hybrid, and the garden is by Julie Toll, in Welwyn Garden City, Hertfordshire.

cleared away, will rot down to form a mushy layer of humus among the gravel, encouraging weeds and spoiling the effect.

One of the most distinctive features of gravel gardens is the extent to which plants will self-sow in them. They do not always do it in the right place or quantity, of course, but unwanted plants are considerably easier to pull from loose gravel than from soil. The scattering effect of self-sown plants creates a feeling of spontaneity that is almost impossible to achieve otherwise.

Gardening in any kind of sun-soaked habitat dominated by drought-tolerant plants needs to take into account the appearance of the plants used. Most importantly, the characteristics of such plants need to be recognized as providing clues to species that may be drought-tolerant. A great many plants of dry habitats are technically sub-shrubs: low, hummock-forming plants

with a dense, much-branched habit and small leaves. These leaves tend to be physically tough, often needle-like, and often covered with a fine layer of hairs or a waxy coating, giving them a grey or silver appearance. The twiggy habit reduces wind velocity and physical damage while the tough, leathery leaves have evolved to reduce desiccation. Grasses of such habitats are nearly always bunch grasses (see pages 41–42) and have fine leaves. True succulents tend to be rare in colder climates. Other common shapes are rosettes of leathery leaves, as in species of yucca and agave. Spiny or thistle-like shapes are also common, and help to deter grazing animals. A great many drought-tolerators are evergreen; these plants need to conserve resources, and that is not achieved by casting leaves to the ground once a year.

A little reflection reveals an intriguing fact: that the dense, twiggy habit so typical of such Mediterranean-

Above and right A gravel garden at Bury Court, a former farmyard in Hampshire, with a background of old agricultural buildings, beams from which have been used to make a sculpture. Planting is by Piet Oudolf. The predominant plant form is the hummock, the result of densely twiggy sub-shrubs growing where they can expand more or less unimpeded in any direction. Such a habit is characteristic of plants from Mediterranean-type – and therefore drought-prone – environments. Nearly all are evergreen, so the year-long display of foliage in a range of green to grey to silver is an especially attractive characteristic. The red–pink *Sedum spectabile* (*above*), which flowers in late summer, is a more spectacularly flowering component of this planting, although it dies back during the winter.

climate shrubs as lavender and cistus is seen again in plants from superficially very different habitats, as in the heathers of the Scottish moorlands or the hebes of the New Zealand mountains. Plants here face the cold but also, more importantly, the wind. Both wind and sun dry plants out, so it should perhaps not be surprising that evolution has driven many to adopt a similar habit in these very different environments. The same is true of fine-leaved bunch grasses.

Having recognized how particular characteristics occur among plants of similar environments, the aware gardener can begin to make predictions about unfamiliar plants, and make leaps of faith concerning the conditions in which they might succeed. It does not at first make much sense to plant species of Mediterranean origin on the windswept coast of northern Scotland. In fact, cold here is not the problem, but constant wind, and many Mediterranean species thrive. Not only does their foliage resist desiccation, but also the resilient twiggy habit means that constant buffeting does them little damage.

Other dry-habitat plants avoid the heat not by resisting it, but by simply disappearing. Species that die down to bulbs and tubers in the heat of the summer are very common in these climates – the richest bulb floras are in the Middle East, Central Asia and western North America. They start to grow as soon as the sun warms the ground, and flower, seed and recharge their storage organs with nutrients before the sun's strength desiccates the soil. Annuals have an even more drastic strategy, tending to germinate with the rains of autumn and then flower and seed in the spring. The parent plant may die with the summer sun, but vast quantities of seed will have been scattered far and wide to provide the next generation.

It should now be clear that the spring and early summer are very colourful in dry habitats. The rest of

the year may see comparatively little flower interest, although the cool of autumn may bring about what is called in some Mediterranean countries 'the second spring'. The lack of flowers, however, is made up for by the fact that the majority of these plants are evergreen, with a wide range of tones, from green to silver. There is also a bonus for those who garden in climates where drought is occasional rather than inevitable: some herbaceous species − *Salvia nemorosa* and *Knautia macedonica* among them − react to good moisture supplies by repeat or constant flowering.

Plant shape is key to creating successful nature-inspired planting combinations for dry sites. Dry-climate shapes tend towards two extremes, the gentle and the dramatic. The hummocky shape of sub-shrubs is somehow immensely satisfying to the human eye, and it can be repeated endlessly without ever jarring. The fine-leaved bunch-grass shape can also be repeated, but at the same time makes a pleasing and gentle contrast with the hummock. Real contrast comes from rosettes and other spiky plants. These are very effective if repeated to create a rhythm. Overdone, however, the effect is restless, even aggressive. Bulbs and annuals make good 'scatter plants', flowering and disappearing among the more permanent elements.

Above all, because dry-habitat plants tend to grow more slowly and in a more compact way than those of lusher habitats, they are more predictable, allowing the gardener a better chance at playing with arranging plants with the confidence that the results will stay put for a while. The wide range of foliage colours shown by these plants is also a great joy to work with.

Plants for Dry Gardens

Right, top *Euphorbia characias* has a growth cycle typical of many Mediterranean-climate plants, growing during the winter and flowering in early spring. Its yellow−green flower colour combines well with the brighter tones of spring bulbs.

Right, bottom One of the grape hyacinths, *Muscari armeniacum*, a group of sun-loving bulbs particularly useful for the natural-style gardener as they readily naturalize, forming colonies of vivid blue in mid- to late spring.

Opposite, top *Eremurus* are dramatic plants from semi-desert areas of Asia, with dramatic flower-packed spires. They are among the few drought-tolerant plants that have such a strong vertical emphasis. They are not the easiest plants to provide for, needing fertile soil and disliking competition, but are very rewarding.

Opposite, bottom left French lavender, *Lavandula stoechas*, is not as hardy as the more familiar lavender species (*L. angustifolia*), but is popular for the distinctive flag-like petals on the flower heads. Like many Mediterranean-climate sub-shrubs, it tends to grow best long-term on lean, stony soils.

Opposite, bottom right Colourful hybrids of achillea flourish on free-draining sandy soils. After blooming in early to midsummer, the flowers fade attractively.

Euphorbia characias

Muscari armeniacum

Eremurus × *isabellinus* 'Cleopatra'

Lavandula stoechas

Achillea sp.

PLANT SELECTION

Choosing appropriate plants is fundamental to success with wild-style gardening. 'Appropriate' means plants that have evolved to flourish in conditions similar to those found in the garden. This does not necessarily mean regionally native species; if an area is naturally dominated by forest, but the garden is open to the full strength of the sun, then locally native shade-loving species will not thrive, and species from outside the region may be ecologically better suited.

Reference books will obviously be the main source of information for researching plants. Seeing what grows well in other gardens locally is another very good way of judging what might thrive; gardens open to the public often provide information aimed at private gardeners. Some of these also put on lectures and workshops. 'Getting a feel' for the local environment is very important, developing an intuitive understanding for the prevailing climate and soil conditions. Garden societies are a valuable way of meeting other gardeners and hearing from expert lecturers.

SITE PREPARATION

Traditional gardening aimed at producing ideal conditions, a fertile, easy-to-work soil that gave bumper crops of fruit, vegetables and flowers. This can be very difficult to achieve, and trying to reach this perfect situation has all too often involved large quantities of materials – fertilizers, peat, manure, grit and so on – being imported into the garden. Simply rejecting this style of gardening avoids many unsustainable and environmentally unfriendly practices. Selecting plants that suit the local environment and therefore do not need soil modification is a major step towards making this break with the past.

Soil modification may be necessary where building operations have resulted in a combination of conditions that make growing any plants difficult: soil compaction, rubble, high alkalinity, an absence of humus (the decayed remains of plants, which does so much to make soil 'plant friendly'). The best cure for such conditions is the application of large quantities of organic matter (well-rotted manure or compost), either dug in or simply applied as a mulch.

The most important aspect of site preparation is the removal of perennial weeds. The exception is where there is an existing selection of wild plants that it is desirable to keep (see page 182). For the most part these weeds are species that would not naturally be present on the site; they are opportunistic travellers, rather like rats, that make the most of the conditions we create to spread voraciously. In some regions, many are invasive non-natives. They tend to reduce biodiversity and can make the establishment of an attractive and rich flora very difficult. The removal of perennial weeds, including all trace of their roots, before you start planting is perhaps the task that will do the most to minimize time-consuming work in the future. The germination of weed seeds will continue to be a problem, but unwanted seedlings are much easier to deal with than regenerating roots.

Perennial weeds can be effectively killed by being smothered with black plastic or old carpet for a year. This is also a good way of encouraging all dead vegetation underneath to decay; as noted above (see page 15), however, there is a disposal problem once the plastic or carpet has done its job. Often it is simpler and quicker to use herbicides; glyphosate-based products are particularly effective and have an excellent safety and environmental record.

SOWING AND ESTABLISHING MEADOWS AND PRAIRIES

Meadows and prairies are both grass-matrix plant communities, with a minority component of wild flowers. In some cases a wild-flower mix only is used. Any reputable supplier of wild-flower seed will provide detailed instructions on how to prepare the ground, sow the seed and care for the plants. They will also advise on timing, which may vary among seed mixes and regions. There are, however, some general procedures.

Ensure that the soil is as free of weed seed as possible, as well as root-free, because weed seedlings will compete with the germinating meadow seedlings. In the case of European meadow mixes this can be easily achieved by stripping off the uppermost layer of topsoil, which will take most of the weed-seed load with it and, as a bonus, help reduce fertility. Establishing meadow is very much easier on lower-fertility soils because the growth of competitive species (wanted or unwanted) is reduced, so allowing slower-growing or less vigorous ones a better chance of success. Where soil removal is not an option, or not desirable, the best way of reducing weed seed is to hoe off or spray weed seedlings as they appear, followed by shallow cultivation of the soil, then remove the next crop of weed seedlings, and so on for a whole growing season, or until there is little more germination. Patience may be required!

Soils for sowing must be broken up as much as possible to form a fine tilth. If the nature of the soil or the weather conditions do not allow this, then consider spreading a layer of sharp sand, 3–5 cm (1½–2 in) deep, over the entire site, and sowing into that. It may be an expensive option, but the advantages are enormous: weed seed is kept buried, germination is easy and rapid in the sand, water pooling during rain is minimized and any weeds that do appear are easily removed.

Irrigation with a sprinkler system may be necessary during the first few months if the weather is dry. It is far better to soak the soil completely in one big watering session than to water little and often, a practice that simply encourages roots to stay near the surface and so become even more vulnerable to drought.

Meadows and prairies need cutting in their first year. This is important as it limits the growth of the most vigorous components (chiefly grasses) and helps allow slower ones to catch up. Cutting should be done whenever the seedlings are taller than 20 cm (8 in). Clippings should ideally be removed from meadows, but can be left on prairies.

Weeding is inadvisable until the second year, as desired seedlings are all too easily removed by mistake.

LONG-TERM MEADOW AND PRAIRIE MANAGEMENT

Meadows and prairies will change their composition during the first few years, as vigorous but short-lived species will tend to dominate at first, to be replaced by long-lived but slow-growing ones. Frequent mowing is recommended if particular species or weeds appear to be getting the upper hand. Once established, meadows can be mown as little as once a year. The best time for mowing is midsummer, the traditional time for cutting hay meadows. Wait until the majority of species have seeded, then cut, removing the clippings if the soil is fertile. Mowing meadows at different frequencies and/or at varying heights can create interesting effects, as different species are favoured by different mowing regimes.

From the third year on, prairies are best burnt annually, during a dry spell in mid-spring, although whether this is done depends on the attitudes of neighbours and the local fire department. Burning destroys or reduces alien weeds, and reduces the growth of the more vigorous components, as well as making space for seedling regeneration. Meadows can also be burnt every few years; although little practised, this is a traditional farming technique that is useful for reducing the tussocky growth of vigorous grasses.

BORDER PLANT MANAGEMENT

Nature-inspired borders need little management once established. The main task is the removal of dead stems, which should be done as late as possible, in order to leave seed for birds over the winter. The easiest way of doing this is with a brush-cutter, leaving the debris as a mulch; it is, however, very untidy! Alternatively, compost the material, cutting long stems into pieces less than 30 cm (1 ft) long. Composting can be slow, which may mean that heaps take up a lot of space. Rotted compost can be returned to the border as mulch or used elsewhere in the garden.

Weed control is important, especially in the early years. In climates with mild winters, unwanted grass and pasture weeds typically begin to grow several months before most ornamental perennials; this creates an opportunity

to control them. The most time-efficient method is to spray them very carefully with a glyphosate-based herbicide. Alternatively, they can be dug out or, if small and the weather is dry or windy, hoed off. Most weed seed germinates from a supply already in the soil, so if soil disturbance is avoided the amount of weed germination will reduce over the years. If weed seeding is a particular problem, consider using a mulch of organic material, such as well-rotted manure or wood chips, around perennials. It will suppress weed seed germination, but may also suppress desired perennials or biennials from regenerating.

Once a planting is established, usually from the third year, a more pragmatic view can be taken towards weeds. Most low-level weeds are not able to compete with vigorous perennials that are taller than they are; even the creeping buttercup (*Ranunculus repens*), which can smother young borders, is little more than a nuisance in many established ones – its yellow flowers are even a bonus! Very small weeds, such as daisies (*Bellis perennis*) or Persian speedwell (*Veronica persica*) are rarely a problem and perhaps should be left. In a very well-established naturalistic border, even such large weeds as the notably aggressive rosebay willowherb (*Chamerion angustifolium*) can be cautiously welcomed, as they make little headway against large clumps of ornamental perennials.

However, perennial clumps may grow too large over time and start to

smother less vigorous plants; geraniums are particularly notorious in this regard. Digging up the plants and dividing them into smaller pieces will be necessary. With time, clumps of most perennials will spread and meet each other, and then begin to form a complex interwoven tapestry. This is the stage where a full canopy of vegetation, similar to that found in most wild habitats, has begun to develop. Its appearance is quite different from that of the conventional border, where bare earth separates one clump from another. From now on, the role of the gardener is to edit and manage a thriving artificial ecosystem.

Those species that spread primarily through seed, rather than vegetatively as an ever-spreading clump, need space for their seedlings to grow. Whether they do or not, and how much they do, is one of the great unpredictabilities of natural-style gardening. As a general rule, perennials and biennials seed most freely in light, sandy soils, and are least likely to in heavy clays. Some species may produce too many seedlings, in which case the excess should be hoed off before they get too big. The ideal situation is that several plants in the planting scheme produce a steady supply of seedlings, and that most of these are short-lived species that would otherwise die out. Quite which species will do this is almost impossible to predict; gardeners are well advised to adopt an attitude of open-minded pragmatism, and to work with the results. There are often some very pleasant surprises.

Seedlings will be most likely to appear in bare ground, and least likely to germinate in places where they have to face strong competition from established plants. It is clear that in established borders where there is little room, there will be relatively few, and that in young borders with gaps there could be a great many. Seeding is particularly pronounced in gravel gardens or between paving slabs, particularly of species that do not seed in ordinary garden conditions. A good example is the soft-looking grass *Stipa tenuissima*, which can form extensive drifts in gravel gardens, creating an attractive meadow-like effect.

A recent development in the management of herbaceous plants is the practice of summer pruning, which in many species encourages the formation of bushier plants bearing a larger head of flowers at a lower height than normal. This could be of great advantage in smaller gardens, where it may be impracticable or undesirable to have tall prairie species. It is most likely to give satisfactory results in climates where summers are hot and wet, and least likely where summers are cool and rainfall unpredictable.

WOODLAND PLANT MANAGEMENT

Young trees and shrubs need more carefully prepared soil than perennials do; in particular, the soil must be broken up around the immediate zone of planting in order to encourage the young roots to spread out. The most common causes of failure are a shortage of water in the first year and competition from grasses, perennials or weeds around the base in the first three years. If shrubs or trees and perennials or wild flowers are to be combined, young woody plants need to be planted in a vegetation-free zone around a metre (or a yard) wide. This even applies to such vigorous species as willows.

Willows, for decoration (see 'Sculpture and Ornament', above), are generally planted as cuttings during the winter or early spring. Rods are simply pushed down into undug soil, and growth will be rapid, especially in moist conditions. Once formed, willow sculptures must be pruned every year, and failure to do so will result in rapid loss of the sculpture's shape. Pruning consists of removing all the current year's shoots at the end of the year.

Most gardeners plant trees and shrubs and then either let them grow or clip them into unnatural, rounded shapes. While the latter practice creates a totally unnatural appearance, a little topiary may combine well with wild planting, as it makes the wildness look intentional. For the most part, though, if applied to every shrub in the garden, the effect is completely unnatural; it also frequently restricts flowering.

'Natural' shrub shapes may also be unsatisfactory, because they are somewhat amorphous. A number of strategies may improve their shape and create possibilities for more adventurous gardening. Cutting away lower branches allows attractive bark or an interesting branching habit to be appreciated, and lets in light to allow for underplanting with early-flowering perennials and bulbs. The coppicing of trees and shrubs (see page 76) is another, more radical, technique, and involves cutting the plant back to the base either every year or every few years. It is a particularly useful way of restricting the growth of vigorous species or those that sucker aggressively. Visually, combining coppiced trees with medium-height or shorter perennials can work very well, particularly if the perennials tolerate some shade.

Many plants of the forest floor have very particular requirements, for a light, humus-rich soil that holds moisture but is at the same time free-draining. Typically, their roots will be limited to a shallow surface layer of such material, the result of many years of decaying leaves, while the tree roots will be further down. It is, however, common practice to sweep up dead leaves, and given that the dead foliage of some species, such as beech (*Fagus*) and maples (*Acer*), decays slowly and smothers ground-level plants, it may be a good idea even for areas of woodland planting. Composting the leaves and returning the resulting dark-brown, humus-rich material as a mulch to woodland plants will help to develop the kind of soil they appreciate.

MANAGING EXISTING WILD OR SEMI-WILD AREAS

In some regions it is common for new houses to be built in areas of pre-existing forest. This is rarely virgin forest, and is most likely to be secondary or tertiary, the result of regeneration after the initial natural tree cover was felled. It may contain a good mix of species and have a varied and interesting ground-level flora. In other places, a new garden, or an area that has been enclosed as an extension to an existing garden, may have what appears to be a varied semi-natural vegetation. Gardeners in such situations may face a quandary: do they leave it and try to manage it, remove it and start again, or try to improve and 'edit' it?

Such an area is best left for a year, in order to see what plant species appear. A local wild-flower guide is perhaps the most important tool during this first year. An attractive and relatively species-rich flora should clearly be largely left alone, with perhaps just some cautious addition of new plants for extra visual impact. However, it will almost certainly need management of some kind.

Attractive biodiverse, semi-natural vegetation is often degraded by the spread of aggressive plant species, which shade out less vigorous ones. Brambles are one of the worst offenders; seedling trees and shrubs, particularly of such pioneer species as birch (*Betula*) and European sycamore (*Acer pseudoplatanus*) can also rapidly shade out more interesting vegetation. Ideally, such plants should be dug out, but on a large scale regular use of a brushcutter to cut them down to ground level will eventually kill them. Once the ground is kept clear in this way, the growth of such woodland floor species as bluebells (*Hyacinthoides non-scripta*) or, in North America, trilliums, can be surprisingly rapid.

In open conditions, the spread of scrubby woody vegetation needs to be controlled, as these plants are among the worst enemies of wild-flower-rich grassland. Another is the growth of vigorous pasture grasses. In north-west Europe, where they are native, they benefit from nitrogen pollution at the expense of many other species; in North America they often suppress native vegetation. A programme of regular mowing or occasional burning will tip the balance in favour of a wider and more interesting flora; once established, this will require mowing only once or twice a year. It should be noted that 'mowing' is not necessarily to be taken literally: a brushcutter or tractor-mounted flail is often better than a grass mower. Ideally, clippings should be removed to reduce fertility.

GROWING YOUR OWN

Naturalistic planting depends for a lot of its impact on there being multiples of a few species. Buying plants from garden centres is always expensive; traditional nurseries or wholesalers are generally much cheaper. The best way is to grow your own from seed. Not only is it very cost-effective, but also it usually ensures much greater genetic variation, which is important if your plants are to self-sow and spread themselves around. Seed germination is a subject in itself, however, as many species have evolved mechanisms to avoid germination in unfavourable conditions or to delay it, sometimes for up to two years. Homework is needed! There are various books available, and the Internet can also be a very useful source of information.

One of the best ways of growing lots of seedlings is in plug trays, whereby up to a hundred young plants grow in individual cells in one plastic tray. Once they have filled the cells it is a very quick job to plant them out, and they will suffer minimal transplanting shock. In some cases, such as in a new border, or large gaps in an existing one, the plugs can go straight into their final positions; otherwise they need to be lined out in a nursery bed to grow on. The plug trays commonly available tend to be quite small, so those who want to grow on large numbers of plants should consider how many are thrown out from wholesale nurseries in the spring. Once cleaned up, they should last the careful gardener at least two years.

'Growing your own', from seed or cutting to mature plant, is a large part of what gardening should be about. There is a deep sense of satisfaction in propagating large numbers of your own plants. In addition, there are practical advantages, as plants that are planted out where they were first grown will be accustomed to the prevailing conditions. There will be a sense that what you have grown truly belongs to the site, so completing the process of making a natural-style garden, a process that begins with deciding what type of vegetation is appropriate for the prevailing conditions. At root, natural-style gardening is about sensitivity to what is appropriate, and an openness to learning – about your site, your plants and the natural places and plant communities that have inspired you.

Gardens to Visit

Many gardens open to the public contain less intensively managed areas, where garden plants form real plant communities, either alone or in conjunction with native plants. The work of designers who have been inspired by natural plant communities, such as Piet Oudolf, James van Sweden or Dan Pearson, is well known, but their work aims to achieve a naturalistic effect rather than create genuinely ecologically functioning plant combinations.

Gardens come and go, and so do the websites that provide information about them. Up-to-date information on the best gardens can be found at noelkingsbury.com/gardens.htm.

UK

Wild-flower meadows are increasingly part of larger gardens open to the public, but there are few examples of the use of a wider flora. Currently, the best example is part of Lady Farm in Somerset (ladyfarm.com). Another very good example is found within surprisingly formal areas at Waltham Place, Berkshire (walthamplace.com). There are small areas at the Eden Project (edenproject.com), and the

Holbrook Garden in Devon has some small very well-planted areas managed as part of a nursery (samshrub.co.uk).

The National Wildlife Centre in Liverpool is a fascinating place to visit for those interested in growing British native plants (wildflower.co.uk).

The Netherlands

There are a large number of public gardens and other spaces where native wild-flower plant communities have been re-created. Those in the parks at Amstelveen, between Amsterdam and Schiphol, are outstanding for many reasons, not least the sophistication of the management. They also take aesthetics into account as well as ecology. The Priona Garden at Slagharen is outstanding, but at the time of writing its future is uncertain (prionatuinen.com).

Germany

Germany, as the homeland of ecology-informed gardening, has many good examples of natural-style gardens, most of them established as part of garden shows and therefore included in large city parks. What gardeners find interesting about the German approach is that

ecological plantings incorporate many conventional garden plants, not just native wild flowers. Munich's Westpark is outstanding; also worth visiting are the Grugapark in Essen and the Palmengarten in Frankfurt am Main. However, far and away the best, and particularly interesting for those with smaller gardens, is Hermannshof in Weinheim (sichtungsgarten-hermannshof.de).

USA

Many botanical gardens contain areas planted with native flora, or preserve areas of native flora. Two of the best are the Crosby Arboretum, Mississippi (crosbyarboretum.msstate.edu), and the San Francisco Botanic Garden (sfbotanicalgarden.org). Some very good native plant communities have been re-created by other bodies, the two best being the Garden in the Woods, Massachusetts (newenglandwildflower.org), and the Lady Bird Johnson Wildflower Center in Texas (wildflower.org).

The prairie, though, is the greatest source of inspiration, plants and knowledge. Although it is commonly associated with the Midwest, prairie is the most

'natural' form of vegetation in open sunny areas over much of the USA. Relict prairies can be seen at the University of Wisconsin Arboretum in Madison (uwarboretum.org), the Morton Arboretum, Illinois (mortonarb.org) and the Missouri Botanical Garden, St Louis (mobot.org). There is a huge area of prairie restoration at the Chicago Botanic Garden, Illinois (chicago-botanic.org).

Two previous books by the author, *The New Perennial Garden* (London: Frances Lincoln 1996) and *Natural Gardening for Small Spaces* (London: Frances Lincoln/ Portland, Ore.: Timber Press 2003), address many of the topics raised above, in particular the application of the science of plant ecology to garden borders and other plantings. One of the most useful books to consider plants as members of communities, and how groups of plants can be chosen for particular environments, is Richard Hansen and Friedrich Stahl, *Perennials and their Garden Habitats* (Cambridge, UK: Cambridge University Press 1993), now unfortunately out of print.

Essay on Gardening (Amsterdam: Architectura & Natura 2008) is an immensely informative account by leading practitioner Henk Gerritsen. For a more conventional guide to herbaceous plants for the contemporary naturalistic garden, two books by Gerritsen and Piet Oudolf are invaluable and written in a lively manner: *Dream Plants for the Natural Garden* (London: Frances Lincoln/Portland, Ore.: Timber Press 2000) and *Planting the Natural Garden* (Portland, Ore.: Timber Press 2003).

Two garden-makers stand out as having an idiosyncratic and extremely successful approach to natural-style gardening. One is Keith Wiley, whose gardening is largely a response to wild plant communities, written up in *On the Wild Side: Experiments in New Naturalism* (Portland, Ore.: Timber Press 2004). The other is Geoffrey Dutton, whose concept of 'marginal gardening' is extremely subtle and who offers many valuable insights, particularly for those gardening in extreme conditions: *Some Branch against the Sky: The Practice and Principles of Marginal Gardening* (Portland, Ore.: Timber Press 1997).

Much of the most interesting work on naturalistic planting has been done in the Department of Landscape at the University of Sheffield by Nigel Dunnett and James Hitchmough; both have written articles in *The Garden* (the journal of the Royal Horticultural Society) and other periodicals. More information can be found on their websites, nigeldunnett.co.uk and shef.ac.uk/landscape/ staff_minisites/james/.

The author is also making information available on his own website, noelkingsbury.com.

Wild flowers and native plants

Much of the work being carried out in ecological horticulture focuses on the native plants of particular regions, and the literature varies from voluminous to non-existent. The best sources of advice — and books — are wild-flower societies, wild-flower gardens or nurseries and seed companies.

UK
Pam Lewis, *Making Wildflower Meadows* (London: Frances Lincoln 2003) is a good narrative account, although the strictly organic approach can make the task unnecessarily difficult.

General guides to growing native wild flowers include Charlotte de la Bédoyère, *Starting Out with Native Plants* (London: New Holland 2007) and Ken Thompson, *No Nettles Required: The Reassuring Truth About Wildlife Gardening* (London: Eden Project Publications 2007). A very good technical guide is *Woodland Wildflowers Work: A Guide to Creative Conservation Techniques for Working in and Developing Woodlands* (Liverpool, UK: Landlife Wildflowers 2005).

North America
The USA has a good network of native-plant societies, thoughtfully collected on a website (newfs.org/ publications-and-media/ resources/native-plant-societies).

Three lively and detailed books for the gardener on North American native plants are all by William Cullina, published by Houghton Mifflin: *The New England Wild Flower Society Guide to Growing and Propagating Wildflowers of the United States and Canada* (2000); *Native Trees, Shrubs, and Vines: A Guide to Using, Growing, and Propagating North American Woody Plants* (2002); and *Native Ferns, Moss and Grasses* (2008).

Finding areas of relict prairie is made easier by Charlotte Adelman and Bernard L. Schwartz, *Prairie Directory of North America* (Wilmette, Ill.: Lawndale Enterprises 2001). Currently the best book on prairie gardening is Sally Wasowski, *Gardening with Prairie Plants: How to Create Beautiful Native Landscapes* (Minneapolis: University of Minnesota Press 2002).

The Lady Bird Johnson Wildflower Center in Texas (see opposite) has an extremely useful regional wild-flower bibliography on its website (wildflower.org/bibliography).

Natural Garden Style happened only because of Nicola Browne's marvellous photographs, taken in an extraordinary range of locations and including such an array of plants. It has been a wonderful experience working with such beautiful material. I should also like to thank Julian Honer, Nicola Bailey, Rosanna Fairhead and everyone else at Merrell who has worked on the project.

The material in this book is the result of many years of research, much of it dependent on the knowledge and goodwill of colleagues and other landscape and horticultural practitioners. I should particularly like to mention Neil Diboll of Prairie Nursery, Wisconsin, for his help with plant identification and for the list of prairie gardens to visit.

As always, I should like to thank my agent, Fiona Lindsay, for her support, and my partner, Jo, with whom I am currently making a garden – negotiating a path between her pots of petunias and my prairie perennials.

First published 2009 by Merrell Publishers Limited

81 Southwark Street
London SE1 0HX

merrellpublishers.com

Text copyright © 2009 Noël Kingsbury
Photography copyright © 2009 Nicola Browne
    unless otherwise credited; see right
Design and layout copyright © 2009 Merrell
    Publishers Limited

All rights reserved. No part of this publication
may be reproduced, stored in a retrieval system
or transmitted, in any form or by any means,
electronic, mechanical, photocopying, recording
or otherwise, without the prior permission in
writing from the publisher.

British Library Cataloguing-in-Publication data:
Kingsbury, Noël
Natural garden style : gardening inspired
by nature
1. Natural gardens – Design
I. Title II. Browne, Nicola
635.9'676

ISBN 978-1-8589-4443-2

Produced by Merrell Publishers Limited
Designed by Martin Lovelock
Jacket designed by Nicola Bailey
Jacket illustration by Angie Lewin; see
    lewin.net/prints
Copy-edited by Caroline Ball
Proof-read by Gordon Lee
Indexed by Diana LeCore

Printed and bound in China

Printed on wood-free paper

PICTURE CREDITS

All photographs copyright © 2009
Nicola Browne except the following:

l = left, r = right, t = top, b = bottom

GAP Photos/Suzie Gibbons: 107tr, 109t,
/Jerry Harpur: 108, /Zara Napier: 104l,
/J.S. Sira: 106, /Rob Whitworth: 107br;
Nicola Browne, courtesy Hannah
Peschar Sculpture Garden/Anthony
Paul (hannahpescharsculpture.com;
anthonypaullandscapedesign.com): 109,
136, 139; Andrea Jones: 102b, 103t;
Andrew Lawson: 116, 117; Clive Nichols:
103br, 106tl; Photolibrary/Howard Rice:
110; © Plantography/Alamy: 105tl

The linocut illustrations throughout
are taken from Angie Lewin's design
for the jacket.

The publisher has made every effort to
trace and contact copyright holders of
the illustrations reproduced in this book;
it will be happy to correct in subsequent
editions any errors or omissions that are
brought to its attention.